A Killing on Ring Jaw Bluff

MERCER
UNIVERSITY PRESS

Endowed by
TOM WATSON BROWN
and
THE WATSON-BROWN FOUNDATION, INC.

A Killing on Ring Jaw Bluff

The Great Recession and the Death
of Small-town Georgia

William Rawlings

Mercer University Press
Macon, Georgia

MUP/ H866

© 2013 Mercer University Press
1400 Coleman Avenue
Macon, Georgia 31207

First Edition

Books published by Mercer University Press are printed on acid-free paper that meets the requirements of the American National Standard for Information Sciences—Permanence of Paper for Printed Library Materials.

Mercer University Press is a member of Green Press Initiative (greenpressinitiative.org), a nonprofit organization working to help publishers and printers increase their use of recycled paper and decrease their use of fiber derived from endangered forests. This book is printed on recycled paper.

ISBN 978-0-88146-431-3

Cataloging-in-Publication Data is available from the Library of Congress

Contents

Author's Preface

I was born and raised in Sandersville, Georgia, where I still live, work, and will probably die and be buried near my father, grandfather, great-grandfather, and the sundry other cousins, uncles, aunts, friends, acquaintances, in-laws, and outlaws who have also called this community home over the past two centuries. Except for the decade or so I spent in various cities receiving an education, my world has been firmly rooted here. Such a stationary life history in twenty-first-century America is increasingly rare, and even more so in that mine is centered in a town whose population has never exceeded seven thousand.

I should make it clear at the outset that I love small Southern towns. I feast on their distinctive histories and revel in the sense of continuity and community that is so often lacking in urban areas. Though the characters, events, and circumstances recounted in this book are unique, they might have been set in any one of dozens—if not hundreds—of similar communities across the rural South. I would request that the reader of this book keep two thoughts in mind. While the story recounts untimely death, I did not intend it as a narrative of murder. And while there are generous helpings of history, this work is not intended to be a definitive account of a pivotal time in Georgia's past. Being neither fish nor fowl, I propose that this is simply an interesting tale, written for the enjoyment of the reader but with the hope that my observations will lead to a better understanding of how things were and why they changed.

This book was the outgrowth of a much-abbreviated version of these events summarized in an article that appeared in the Autumn 2009 issue of *Georgia Backroads* magazine. Searching for an interesting topic in Georgia history, I decided to write about my infamous Great-uncle Charlie who spent a number of his later years in prison, convicted of murdering his first cousin for the insurance proceeds. The killing that took place on Ring Jaw Bluff along the Oconee River on that overcast day in February 1925 was a source of great family embarrassment. The event and the trials that followed made front-page headlines for months in every major newspaper in the state.

Most of what I knew of the case came from my grandmother, the second (and much younger) wife of my grandfather, Benjamin Tar-button Rawlings. She described her brother-in-law as an evil man whose avarice made him capable of anything, including murder. My father, who was twenty years old when C. G. Rawlings died, was a bit more sanguine but still spoke of his uncle as being driven by desperation to commit this ultimate sin. Neither my grandmother nor my father had closely examined the facts of the case.

My original idea was to write a morality tale, a story of a very rich man on the edge of spectacular failure. The exposure of his murder plot and his imprisonment would be exemplars of the wages of sin. I imagined the final piece as an early twentieth-century version of John DeLorean and the suitcase of cocaine. In the end, what I discovered amazed me and totally changed the direction of the story I thought I knew.

You see, my grandmother's (and father's) versions were colored by fact that she was the second wife of a wealthy and much older man, making her the same age or younger than her stepchildren. My father was born nine months to the day after their wedding, and the children of the first marriage shunned the new wife and her spawn. My grandfather died when my father was three, leaving my grandmother to struggle alone as a single parent through the economic turbulence of the 1920s and 1930s. Naturally, her perceptions of the entire Rawlings clan were less than positive. Given this history, I began to explore the past with an unconscious bias, and with the mistaken belief that the facts as they had been presented to me were correct.

As I dug deeper into the events of 1925, my perception of the story began to change. I discovered accounts of the killings of 1893 and the murders of 1906. Most important, I was given access to a transcript of the 1925 trial of J. J. Tanner, Rawlings's overseer and alleged accomplice. What had at first seemed black and white gradually morphed into shades of gray. More significant for this book, however, was my recognition that I did not really understand the events and characters that had shaped the world in which I grew up.

I was vaguely aware that the boll weevil was said to have toppled King Cotton, but I had not realized the importance of the Great Recession of 1920–1921. I had heard that the decade of the 1920s was one of economic collapse and wrenching social change for the agricultural South, but I had no idea of the true magnitude of the transformation. I knew that I had grown up in a once thriving small town now seemingly bypassed by progress, but I did not understand why this had happened.

To say that the killing of Gus Tarbutton was a controversial event would be an understatement of the first order. It had all the right elements for a Greek tragedy: power, wealth, greed, deception, and murder. The various actors in the cast of characters were either flawed or innocent, each in his own way. There was talk of lynch mobs, and the trials that followed were great spectacles, attracting crowds of hundreds. Some of the courtroom dialogue might have been snatched from the works of Erle Stanley Gardner. In the end there was justice, or injustice, depending on how one reads the known facts.

More important to this account, however, was the era in which these events took place. The eternal and insoluble argument as to whether history is driven by events or persons comes to the fore when one begins to examine the social, economic, and political structure of Georgia in the late nineteenth and early twentieth centuries. Were men like Charlie Rawlings and Gus Tarbutton products of their environment, or did they in fact create the environment in which they lived? No doubt the best answer lies somewhere between these extremes. I will leave it to the reader to draw his or her own conclusions.

Despite whatever role such forces, persons, or events may have played in shaping the landscape of those years, the beginning of the end of the dominance of small-town Georgia was well under way by the third decade of the twentieth century. That is the second and more important theme of this book. The bubble in cotton prices during and following World War I, hyperinflation in 1916–1920 followed immediately by the Great Recession and extreme economic deflation, the arrival of the boll weevil, and the unsustainable system of tenant farming were among the factors that led to an implosion of the agricultural economy. This in turn was followed by an accelerated depopulation of rural areas and the widespread collapse of the financial system that had led to the growth of rural villages and towns.

The truth is that for the purpose of this tale, persons and events are so inextricably entwined that it is impossible to separate them. Hence I present this account as an interesting tale, nothing more or less. I will leave it to the reader to take away whatever lessons he or she chooses as important.

William Rawlings
Sandersville, Georgia
September 2011

Introduction

The casual traveler who strays from the main traffic arteries connecting one urban area of the South to another may discover a strange and unusual world. Dotted across the landscape every thirty miles or so are small towns whose reason for existence far from the commerce of modern life seems to defy logic. Their shady streets, lined by massive homes, radiate from decaying village centers with shuttered stores and once majestic buildings slipping shabbily into ruin. Here and there across the countryside, brick or stone chimneys mark the remains of decayed tenant houses, long ago deserted by their former residents. Every now and then, one encounters an abandoned railway line with a local passenger terminal or perhaps a once-grand hotel, suggesting that at some point in the past these places were centers of commerce and affluence.

Indeed, they were. For the first decades of the twentieth century, much of the power and wealth of the South lay not in its cities—themselves often little more than overgrown small towns—but in thriving rural communities scattered across an agricultural landscape whose riches could in large part trace their roots to the production of cotton. But something changed, and with it changed the social, demographic, and economic structure of an entire region. In Georgia, the third decade of the century marked the beginning of the end for many of the state's rural communities. This trend accelerated with time such that now, only a relatively small fraction of the population lives in non-urban areas.

At one point, Georgia was at the center of cotton production, a crop that yielded vast wealth made possible only by intolerable schemes of human labor. The popular myth holds that the system was destroyed by the Mexican boll weevil, which arrived in the state in 1915. With decimation of the cotton crop, especially beginning in 1921 and the years that followed, the economic crisis spread from farmers to merchants to banks, erasing the status quo and the necessary infrastructure that had so richly rewarded the fortunate few. Or so the story goes.

The truth is far more complex. The demise of Georgia's small towns was in large part brought about by the failure of an economic system that was highly dependent on a single crop, but the boll weevil, while holding the potential for devastation, was only one of a number of contributing factors. Its role was—as much as anything—that of delivering a final blow to an already moribund economic and social structure. Should the weevil have arrived a decade earlier or a decade later, it seems likely that its ultimate effects would have been quite different.

This work focuses on two intertwined tales, that of the economic growth and subsequent collapse of rural Georgia's economy during the period between 1910 and 1925, and the story of Charles Graves Rawlings, a wealthy landowner, farmer, businessman, and banker who was convicted of the murder of his first cousin, allegedly to save his struggling bank and personal fortune in a time of economic crisis. The arc of Rawlings's life followed that of the cotton economy in Georgia after the Civil War. As a prominent banker, he participated in the decision of the United States Treasury to effectively monetize cotton, which was a major factor in the economic collapse that followed. He benefited from the bubble in cotton prices that accompanied the World War I era but seemingly ignored the corrosive effects of inflation on the true value of his wealth. As African Americans fled the racism of the South in the years following the war, depleting the labor pool, Rawlings was accused of peonage—involuntary servitude of his farm workers. At a time of wrenching social change, he violated the perceived social mores, and as a consequence he suffered at the hands of the powerful Ku Klux Klan. Eventually, as his world seemed to collapse around him, he was convicted of a murder that he may not have committed.

History is written in retrospect. From the perspective of time, it is clear that the second and third decades of the twentieth century were pivotal for Georgia. A once-powerful agricultural base stumbled, leading to profound demographic, economic, political, and social changes in the years that followed. While much of the United States would enjoy a period of economic abundance in the 1920s, the Great Depression that would eventually engulf the country had begun in the rural South nearly a decade earlier.

A Prosperous Town

A visitor standing on the front lawn of the Methodist church in the east-central Georgia town of Sandersville in late February 1925 might have thought this a prosperous community, one with both a distinguished history and a bright future. The church, crafted of red brick with polished marble accents and a suitable number of stained-glass windows, faced the main east-west highway, appropriately named Church Street but as yet unpaved. Directly across the street stood a simple, white frame house on whose porch the body of a dead Confederate cavalryman had lain, killed in a skirmish during Sherman's March to the Sea in November 1864.

A few hundred feet to the west of the church, a small forest of white marble monuments sprouted from the Old City Cemetery, their sheer quantity and ornateness confirming the fact that Sandersville had produced a significant number of citizens who felt their wealth should be on display long after having shed their mortal coils. Just inside the cemetery entrance that faced the church, two family plots lay on either side of the wagon path. To the left, Rawlings. To the right, Tarbutton. A freshly covered grave in the Tarbutton plot awaited its permanent tombstone.

A block to the east, the spire of the First Baptist Church loomed over the intersection of Church and Harris streets, the latter being the local name for the main north-south highway through the town. On the opposite side of the intersection, a large white Victorian house dominated the crossroads, its location and size a testament to the wealth of its owner. A broad, covered porch lined with turned balusters was shaded from the harsh afternoon sun by two huge magnolia trees. The ornate door opened into a wide hall lined with raised-panel walnut, its glass window etched with the initials "CGR," for Charles Graves Rawlings, the home's owner. It was in this home that on the night of February 18, 1925, Rawlings was arrested for the murder of his first cousin, George Augustus Tarbutton.

News of the arrest of one of Sandersville's most prominent citizens spread rapidly. Five years earlier, it might have seemed incredible that a man of his wealth, power, and influence could even be suspected of such a crime, much less charged with it, but the world had changed. The heady days of easy money and seemingly limitless economic expansion appeared lost forever, and perhaps this was simply one more sign of the new reality.

The facts of the case seemed simple enough. Charlie Rawlings had been, and probably still was, the wealthiest man in the area. But his fortune, like those of many others in Georgia's cotton-producing Black Belt,[1] was closely tied to the farm economy. The sudden drop in cotton prices in 1920 and the ensuing implosion of the infrastructure that had supported the cotton culture spared no one, rich or poor. Like many others of the entrepreneurial class, Rawlings was deeply in debt. He was said to be close to his cousin, but the cousin was

---

[1] The term "Black Belt," used in a geographic sense, refers to a broad crescent-shaped swath of land stretching from Virginia to Mississippi that was the historical center of upland cotton production in the United States. Although the term may have originally applied to soil type in certain areas, in general usage counties of this region have a large African-American population.

heavily insured with the policies payable to Rawlings's struggling bank. There had been an accident—or so they said—some twenty miles away near the river at a place called Ring Jaw Bluff. Tarbutton had been shot in the head. A coroner's jury heard testimony that cast doubt on Rawlings's account of the tragedy. He was ordered arrested on a preliminary charge of murder.

While some may have been shocked at the news, others may have felt a quiet sense of gloating, for there was another side to Charlie Rawlings. He was a man who had stepped on a number of people on his way up. Someone who always seemed to avoid the well-deserved consequences of his many sins and transgressions. Someone who had gotten away with too much for too long. Perhaps this time would be different.

For many, it was hoped that the new year, 1925, would bring change. It was the beginning of the sixth year of the lingering uncertainty. Men of substance and property, formerly assured of their wealth and place in the evolving century, were now doubtful of their future. While the rest of the nation was in the midst of what would be known as the "Roaring Twenties," the mood was grim in small towns across the South. The construction of the big houses that lined Main Streets had ground to an abrupt halt. Nearly half the state's banks had failed. Farmers and merchants alike were facing bankruptcy. Farms were abandoned as steward sharecroppers migrated to the growing cities, often under cover of darkness, hoping to avoid their unpaid creditors. The Klan rallied and railed about America's moral decay, eager to assign blame for events seemingly beyond anyone's control.

So in some ways, the arrest of Charlie Rawlings may have been a sign of the times, a bit of concrete evidence that the old order was dead and a new one would soon arise. But this story, while unique to one small east-central Georgia town, was in many ways similar to others being played out in towns and villages across the vast lands of the cotton-producing South. The details and the characters may have been different, but the basic theme was the same. The world was changing, and with it small towns were dying.

2

A Self-made Man

Charlie Rawlings was rich. Not the ordinary kind of rich that merely allowed him to live comfortably, but rather the sort of wealth that most men could only dream of accumulating in their lifetimes. He was not unique. He was a wealthy man in a wealthy town, one of a dozen or more who had managed to overcome and persevere while hanging on to the fruits of a lifetime of work. Now, nearly sixty-seven years of age, he was facing a charge of murder and, if convicted, the prospect of spending his final years in prison or, worse, his final seconds in the state's new electric chair.

His home, grand as it might be, was one of many similar homes that lined Harris Street, known locally as "Silk Stocking Street" for the lofty lifestyles of its residents. Fortunes made in cotton, in banking, in warehouses, and in railroads had paid for spacious Victorian mansions adorned with wide porches and ornate fretwork. The famous architect, Charles Choate, had designed and built more than a few. While one home might be known as that of the banker or another as that of the plantation owner, it could be said that Charlie Rawlings had it all. He reputedly owned more than thirty thousand acres of cropland and timberland. He owned a bank he had founded nearly two decades earlier. He was the majority shareholder and president of the local railroad. He owned a hotel, gins, warehouses, and other businesses.

He intended to face this latest challenge, this accusation of the murder of a man with whom he had been quite close, like he had faced all the others. He intended to win, to be exonerated, to walk away unscathed as he had before. But it is hard not to imagine that he knew the stakes were higher this time. Charlie Rawlings was no longer the young man who had set out to build an empire, his life before him and the world a bazaar of unlimited opportunity. His businesses were struggling. His children were grown and married. His wife had been dead for more than three years. His brothers had turned against him in a dispute over their father's estate. He had his friends and those who believed in his innocence, but the accusation of the murder of his widely respected first cousin had severed any support he might have expected from his mother's side of the family.

The man whom Charlie was accused of killing was a first cousin, but their relationship was more than that. George Augustus Tarbutton, known simply as "Gus," was born in 1875. His father died when he was five, followed by his mother two years later. At age fourteen, he came to live with his Aunt Soonie and Uncle Fred, Charlie's parents. Despite the differences in their ages, Gus and Charlie seemed to find a mutual bond. As Charlie would say later, "I loved him like a son." Charlie assumed the role of Gus's mentor and surrogate older brother, acting as legal guardian for his inheritance, helping set him up in the farming business, and even introducing him to his future wife. By all reports, they were very close, not only as blood relatives but as friends and business associates.

Charlie Rawlings was born in May 1858 on his father's cotton plantation near Sandersville, one of four sons among seven children. The Rawlings had migrated to Georgia from Virginia at the beginning of the nineteenth century. They settled in Washington County, then a long swath of former

Indian territory stretching from near modern-day Athens to coastal Liberty County, bounded on the east by the Ogeechee and Canoochee rivers and on the west by the Oconee and Altamaha. His grandfather, a surveyor by trade, "became a prominent and influential citizen, amassing a great acreage of plantations and owning many slaves."[1] His father Frederick, born in 1821, was a successful cotton planter, having twenty-nine slaves on the cusp of the Civil War.[2] Like many of his generation, Frederick served in the Confederate military, only to see his farms destroyed by Sherman's scorched earth campaign on the March to the Sea. Charlie's mother, born Susan Tarbutton, was from another prominent and well-respected Washington County family.

By the time of Charlie's birth, Washington County had shrunken considerably in size, its northern and southern extremities carved off to form bits and pieces of a dozen other counties as multiple small towns sprang up across the agricultural landscape. Later that same year, Johnson County, with its county seat of Wrightsville, was formed out of land ceded from Washington, Emanuel, and Laurens counties. More than a half century later, Charlie would become the largest landowner in Johnson County.

In Washington County, the dusty crossroads town of Sandersville had become the county seat. By the 1830s, it boasted of a fine two-story brick courthouse, with a few stores and saloons surrounding it on the muddy city square. In the early 1840s, the railroad connecting Savannah to Marthasville (later Atlanta) had punched its way through from the coast. Fearing the effect of the smoke-belching mechanical monster, the city fathers decreed that the line should be placed no closer than

---

[1] Knight 1917, 3146.
[2] 1860 United States Census.

three miles from the courthouse, resulting in the new settlement of Tennille exactly three miles to the south.

Though reduced in size, Washington County was ideally located to take advantage of the state's growing economy. Sitting astride the geologic Fall Line, the land to the north was gently rolling, with red clay hills topped by sandy soil and cut by rock-bottomed, straight-flowing rivers. Here timber grew well on the hillsides and in the bottoms, while cotton thrived on the mule-terraced areas in between. In the south of the county and extending on toward Wrightsville and beyond, the land lay in the northern edge of the Coastal Plain, where lazy rivers meandered their way to the sea through wide, timber-rich lowlands, with vast areas of relatively flat cropland covering the countryside.

Roads, which were often nearly impassable in the best of times, were secondary to the railroads when it came to transportation of crops, animals, and farm supplies. Though Sherman's men had destroyed mile after mile of track, the lines were rapidly rebuilt after the war. By the latter third of the nineteenth century, Tennille had become a major railroad terminus, with short-line tracks extending north and south and connecting to the main lines for the seaports of the coast and beyond. Cheap labor, good transportation, a long growing season, and the abundant natural resources of land, timber, and water led entrepreneurs and businessmen to fortunes in agriculture, manufacturing, and the support services they required. It was into this world that Charlie Rawlings set out to make his fortune.

His two older brothers pursued highly successful careers in medicine and law. William, born in 1850, attended Emory College before receiving his medical training at the University of Maryland and in Europe. He opened one of the first private hospitals in middle Georgia, soon achieving national reputation for his skill as a surgeon. Ben, born two years later, also attended Emory before studying law and returning to Sandersville to open a thriving practice. Both men had extensive agricultural interests, each owning thousands of acres of land. Both earned wide respect in their community and at various times represented Washington County in the state legislature.

Charlie chose a different path. He left home early and by age twenty-one was living in a boarding house, his occupation listed as liveryman. By the mid-1880s he owned his own livery stable, selling horses and mules to meet the ever-increasing demand of farmers and plantation owners. He did his civic duty, serving at least two terms on Sandersville's City Council, and on county juries. As his older brothers' reputations in medicine and law grew, Charlie was wheeling and dealing in the world of business, quietly doing whatever it took to acquire wealth. While education might demand respect and bestow power, money worked equally well.

In 1888, Charlie married Tallulah Perkins, the eighteen-year-old daughter of a prominent lumberman. "Lula" was said to be pretty and vivacious, and over the coming years she would provide him with two sons and three daughters. His oldest son, the one he chose to name Charles Graves Rawlings, died in early childhood. The others went on to lead long and successful lives.

Life in the rural South of the late nineteenth century represents a unique era in American history. The population was scattered about in small towns and villages, physically and socially separated from one another. The cycle of the year revolved around the agricultural calendar, as the livelihood of the vast majority of families was directly or indirectly tied to it. The social structure was divided into a strict, if somewhat flexible, pecking order. At the top were the merchants, bankers, brokers, and businessmen who controlled the flow of goods, capital, and, most important, credit. Next were the landowners, who controlled the primary means of production. These two groups often overlapped in their membership, and their economic fates were inextricably intertwined. Below this were the tenant farmers, a class that grew steadily following the Civil War until it included the majority of all farmers by the third decade of the twentieth century.

Race and gender were all important. For practical purposes, the black population, which represented the majority of citizens in many cotton-producing counties, was disenfranchised and held in economic servitude to the landowners and capitalists who often considered them little more than chattel. With this said, however, they were an absolute necessity as a source of labor and an integral part of the economic system, as events would later prove. The lot of women was scarcely better. Unable to vote, and for many years legally subservient to their husbands or male relatives, they managed the household, became field hands at harvest time, bore multiple children, and often died young.

Towns, even those separated by a few miles of rutted road, viewed each other with deep suspicion. Sandersville and Tennille, for example, only three miles distant, were constant rivals. Despite often close family or business connections, the general feeling was that "those people" in the other town were somehow a little different, a little peculiar, and perhaps not as forthright or trustworthy as one's local friends, neighbors, or relatives. The sense of suspicion and distrust was magnified proportionate to the distance. As many—perhaps the majority—of people rarely traveled outside the county, towns thirty or more miles away were often considered to have an entirely different ethos. This was reinforced by subtle but distinct regional differences in accents. Citizens of Wrightsville and Sandersville, though living only nineteen miles apart, had (and still have) slight variations in the pronunciation of certain words.

The system, as it evolved, favored the haves over the have-nots. The law was often flexible, or flexibly applied. At various times, it seemed that everyone from juries to judges could be bought. Despite local prohibition laws, candidates dispensed "election liquor" freely to purchase votes. It was in this environment that a man with a yen for success and the willingness to bend the rules could triumph. Charlie Rawlings thrived in this environment.

The society that existed in the late 1800s and early 1900s was the product of more than a century of social evolution. To fully understand the hows and whys of its genesis, one must understand the forces that shaped it. These can be summarized in one word: cotton.

3

The Land of Cotton

In the late 1970s, the British Broadcasting Corporation produced a series of television documentaries titled *Connections*, written and presented by science historian James Burke. Burke took a somewhat unconventional and non-teleological view of history, drawing associations between seemingly unrelated events and their influence on the subsequent course of human society. If one were to follow Burke's thesis, it would be reasonable to attribute many of the positive and negative events in United States history on Eli Whitney, inventor of the cotton gin.

To be fair, Whitney did not so much invent the gin[1] as redesign and perfect its concept during a 1793 stay on a Georgia plantation near Savannah. Mechanical devices that separated cotton's seeds from its fibers had been used for more than a millennium in parts of Asia.[2] Within a few years, Whitney's first crude model had been extensively modified and improved by others who would reap the fortunes that eluded its nominal inventor. It was this seminal event, however, that made widespread cotton production economically feasible and led to—again following Burke's non-linear view of history—the rise and persistence of slavery in the United States, the ability of this country to survive as an independent nation, the American Civil War, the distinct culture of the South as we

---

[1] The word "gin" is used as both a noun and a verb and is said to be a variant of "engine," tracing its roots to Middle English.

[2] Scherer 1916, 19.

know it, and the rise and fall of small towns across the region. American cotton's role on the world stage helped assure Great Britain's economic dominance in the nineteenth century while enriching Boston's Brahmins and New York's bankers.

The lingering influence of the cotton culture permeates American life, especially in the South. We speak of having "a tough row to hoe" or of being "in high cotton." If things are going reasonably well, we're "fair to middling," the latter term referring to the average "middle" grade of cotton. We dress in denim, cotton's quintessential fabric. Our dietary tastes are derived in part from the culture of the African slaves who made cotton production possible. We feast on yams, the essence of sweet potato pie.[3] We eat grits and black-eyed peas and okra, the latter a relative of the cotton plant. The oil derived from cottonseeds, incongruously labeled as "vegetable oil," was the original main ingredient of Wesson Oil, Ivory Soap, and Crisco, whose name was cobbled from "*cry*stallized *co*ttonseed oil."[4]

Prized for its fibers that can be spun into thread and woven into cloth, cotton has been used by mankind for more than 5,000 years. There are more than thirty varieties[5] worldwide, most of which have no commercial application. Domesticated cotton is a member of the swamp mallow family. Four types, two in the Old World and two in the New, have fibers

---

[3] Although the terms "yam" and "sweet potato" are commonly used interchangeably in the South, they are quite different and unrelated tubers. The yam lent its name to the American sweet potato via slaves brought from West Africa, where the yam is a common food staple. Although there is a vague resemblance between the two tubers, the yam has rough skin and starchy yellowish or white flesh, versus the smooth skin and sweet orange flesh of the potato variety. In Georgia, what are called "yams" are in fact sweet potatoes.

[4] National Cotton Producers Association n.d.

[5] Porcher and Fick 2005.

suitable for use in cloth manufacture. In the Americas, both long-staple *Gossypium barbadense*, known as Sea Island cotton, and medium-staple upland cotton (*Gossypium hirsutum*) trace their genetic roots to Central and South America.

Sea Island cotton is among the finest of fibers, its long, fine strands easily woven into delicate fabrics. But it is finicky, growing well only in a narrow band along the southern coast, as American planters discovered in the eighteenth century. However, its green-seeded cousin, upland cotton, is quite capable of thriving in all sorts of soils, from the rolling red hills of the Piedmont to the sandy flat fields of the inland coastal plain. But there is one major problem. While Sea Island cotton is easily separated from its small black seeds, the fibers of upland cotton stick to theirs tightly.

By the 1790s, a small and prosperous market had developed for Sea Island cotton, but growing the hardier upland variety was economically infeasible. Adaptations of the roller gins used since antiquity were adequate for removing the seeds from Sea Island cotton,[6] but with the potentially more prolific upland variety, this tedious work had to be done by hand. A slave—an integral part of the labor force on many of the South's coastal plantations—could only separate about a pound of upland cotton lint from its seeds in one working day. To produce the now-standard 500-pound bale of this variety would have taken significantly more than a year of one man's labor.

This problem was presented to twenty-seven-year-old Eli Whitney, a Yale graduate who at the time was an itinerant tutor visiting Mulberry Grove, the coastal plantation of the late General Nathaniel Greene. The story is told that the difficulty of separating upland cotton's fibers from its seeds was

---

[6] Ibid.

discussed over dinner one evening. Whitney volunteered to see if he could solve the problem, and within months he had crafted a working model of a gin. With this new mechanical device that used hooks to pull the fibers from the seeds, one slave could now clean up to fifty pounds of cotton in a single day, suddenly making widespread production of upland cotton an economic reality.

Within a few years, the entire nature of farming in the South had changed. Whitney's design was simple and therefore easily copied for free, despite a patent signed by George Washington himself. The basic technology, improved and modified by others, spread rapidly. By 1796, a gin was in operation in Washington County,[7] an area soon destined to be the heart of Georgia's cotton country. Across the settled areas of the southern states, trees were felled, land was cleared, and slaves were bought to attend to the hoeing, chopping, and harvesting of this new money crop.

To understand the growth of small towns in Georgia, one must first understand what was happening in England in the latter part of the eighteenth century. In the Midlands, the Industrial Revolution was in its heyday. Arkwright's spinning jenny coupled with Cartwright's power loom had streamlined the former cottage industries of spinning and weaving into processes of mass production. For the most part, the cloth produced by English factories was woven from wool or flax. Finely woven cotton fabrics were imported from Asia and often in such demand that they were preferred to silk. Cotton was available from India and Africa, but its fibers were short and brittle, making domestic production of cloth from these sources difficult and expensive. With large quantities of quality

---

[7] Jordan 1989.

trans-Atlantic cotton suddenly available, the output of England's mills switched to follow this profitable market.

While some of the newly abundant southern cotton was used domestically in America, most of it was funneled into the export market, feeding the ever-increasing demand of England's mills. In 1793, the year before the newly efficient gin came into use, some 487,000 pounds of cotton were exported to England from the South. A scant seven years later, this figure had risen to 17.8 million pounds, and by 1820 it reached nearly 128 million pounds.[8] The overwhelming majority of this was green-seeded upland cotton ginned by the successors to Whitney's original machine. The numbers continued to grow. By the 1850s, America was supplying 80 percent of Britain's cotton and two-thirds of that used in the world.[9]

The export market for cotton initially defined and continued to encourage a distinct way of life that characterized the South. The trends that emerged shaped American society for the next two centuries. First and foremost was the divergence of southern and northern cultures. Over the coming decades, the North focused on industry, while the South turned to agriculture. Inextricably connected to this shift was the growth and persistence of the institution of slavery, considered a necessary evil by those who profited from it. And there was the relationship with the economically dominant North, one that several historians have described as reducing the South to a "colonial status."[10] Together these factors sculpted the overarching themes of southern life and culture until late in the twentieth century.

---

[8] Yaffa 2005.
[9] Ibid.
[10] Eaton 1961, 196.

Cotton was soon profitable on a scale previously unknown in the Americas. The lure of riches opened new croplands to the west. By 1830, the total cotton production of the states of Georgia, North and South Carolina, and Virginia had been surpassed by that from new plantations in Tennessee, Louisiana, Alabama, and Mississippi.[11] The South's nascent manufacturing industry was quickly abandoned in favor of cotton. Production of the traditional crops of tobacco, flax, indigo, and rice fell sharply.[12] As international demand for cotton as a commodity increased, the American South carved out a near-monopoly not dissimilar to that of the oil-producing Middle East a century and a half later.

In the North, meanwhile, the spinning and weaving industries grew rapidly. Using designs modeled after those used in England, the mills of Massachusetts, formerly devoted to wool, turned to the abundant supply of domestically produced cotton. These mills, manned at first by local country-folk-come-to-town and later by wage-earning European immigrants, fostered a society quite different from that of the South, which depended in large part on African-rooted slave labor.

More than any other single factor, this diversification of economies set the South and North on different paths of population distribution. Agriculture, almost by definition, requires large blocks of land managed by relatively few people. Industry, particularly the type represented by factories, requires little land but an intense concentration of workers. Thus for the next century or more, the South's abundant lands were diffusely populated in support of the cotton culture, while in the North, the predominant growth pattern was that of cities.

---

[11] Yaffa 2005.
[12] Scherer 1916.

The most striking trend, however, and that which would nearly tear the country asunder, was the growth of slavery in the South. While allowed on a limited basis under the Constitution, the institution was considered an abomination by many. It had a firm, if ambivalent, place in the new nation's culture, however, and even the abolitionists counted a number of prominent slave owners among their ranks. It seems to be the general consensus of historians that the institution of slavery would have died a quiet and ignoble death early in the nineteenth century were it not for cotton. Or, alternatively, it might be more correct to say it would have died were it not for the lure of riches made possible through cotton production. Morality aside, providing for the sustenance of slaves could be justified only if the products of their labors exceeded the cost of their upkeep. With cotton, there was no question of this.

In 1790, prior to Whitney's invention of the gin, the state of New York counted 21,324 slaves among its inhabitants.[13] Georgia had 29,264. Some twenty years later, New York's slave population had fallen to just above 15,000, while Georgia's had more than tripled to 105,218. By 1860, the number of slaves in the United States had grown to nearly four million,[14] the majority of whom were directly involved in cotton production in the South. Because of cotton, the South became rich. By 1860, Georgia led the nation in personal wealth,[15] much of which was accounted for by the value of slaves, who in turn were valuable as a necessary part of the agricultural system.

---

[13] Ibid., 150ff.
[14] United States Census 1860.
[15] Range 1954.

The relationship between the North and the South as the nineteenth century progressed was eloquently summarized by one historian[16] writing in 1916:

> Thus the Industrial Revolution in England cooperated with an unexampled cotton production in America to bring about the political revolution of the United States. The South, becoming suddenly rich and solidified through the sale to British mills of its huge slave-produced crop, abandoned manufacture to become an enormous plantation. New England, on the other hand, having succeeded at last in acquiring possession of the machinery that had revolutionized England, took enough of the new Southern crop to keep its spindles profitably busy, and led the rest of the North in the development of manufacturing enterprise. Two great sections emerged, more and more socially divergent through the ramifying influences of slavery, and with opposed economic interests due largely to the fact that while one section farmed a certain plant, the other manufactured it.

In commerce, the adage "It takes money to make money" pertains especially to agriculture. Most crops are seasonal, with most of the production costs spent long before harvest. Many agricultural products are traded as commodities, subject to rapid, erratic, and often unpredictable deviations in price. On top of this, there are problems of marketing, transportation, and distribution. These economic uncertainties apply equally to cotton. The banking, shipping, and commodity markets of nineteenth-century America were centered in the northeast, and those involved in them were more than happy to interpose themselves in the supply chain that led from southern fields to English mills.

---

[16] Scherer 1916.

Northern businessmen and bankers, for all their moral righteousness and abhorrence of slavery, were quite willing to act as financiers, intermediaries, and brokers for southern imports and exports, taking "a lion's share of the profits of Southern agriculture."[17] Cotton was bought and sold as eagerly in New York as it was in Memphis or New Orleans. New York banks and Yankee cotton factors loaned to plantation owners. New England shipping fleets carried the South's cotton to ports in England, commonly stopping in New York. As events evolved in the antebellum era, the relationship of the industrial and financial North to the agricultural South resembled that of a mother country to one of its colonies. The resources of the South—plentiful land, comparatively mild weather, and cheap labor—provided abundant and relatively inexpensive raw material for the mills of the northeast. The northern ships that transported southern cotton to Europe brought back luxury items to be sold—at an appropriate profit—to wealthy south-ern planters. Fees, commissions, and the ability to control and manipulate the market added financial incentive. For half a century or more, everyone seemed content to maintain the relationship, and with it the status quo.

For whatever negatives the cotton industry produced, it had a positive side. Cotton became America's leading export and played a vital role in maintaining a positive balance of trade for the new republic. Between the first decade of the nineteenth century and the industrialization that accompanied the start of World War II, cotton held this position, freeing America from becoming a debtor nation by accounting for most of the nation's positive balance of trade.[18]

---

[17] Eaton 1961, 196.
[18] Dattel 2009.

The controversies and compromises that eventually led to the Civil War are often framed in terms of states' rights and the issue of slavery. Underlying these causes, however, were the economics of cotton. The South, via its production of this valuable international commodity, was wealthy. Commerce in the North depended on this wealth. On March 4, 1858, on the cusp of the war and during the debate on the admission of Kansas to the Union, Senator James Henry Hammond of South Carolina delivered his famous "Cotton is King" speech in which he pointed out that the South—based on its cotton exports alone—was economically capable of surviving and thriving as an independent nation.[19] A month later, on a Georgia cotton plantation some 500 miles to the south, Charles Graves Rawlings, who would make his fortune in cotton, was born as the seventh and youngest child of Frederick and Susan Tarbutton Rawlings. Three years later on April 12, 1861, Confederate forces under the command of Brigadier General P. G. T. Beauregard fired the first shots of the Civil War on Fort Sumter in Charleston harbor.

---

[19] Scherer 1916.

4

The Long Depression

On December 21, 1886, Henry W. Grady, the dynamic young editor of the *Atlanta Constitution*, delivered a speech before a banquet of the New England Club in New York City. In his short tenure with Atlanta's leading newspaper, Grady had become known as a tireless cheerleader for the so-called "New South," the name given to his speech that evening before an audience that included many who had led the North to victory a scant two decades earlier. He painted a picture of a society in the midst of transformation, eager to match its former foes in the realms of business and manufacturing, a changed land. But he also spoke of the Old South, its unique identity, and the attachment of its former soldiers to the land, citing the returning veteran who remarked, "You may leave the South if you want to, but I am going to Sandersville, kiss my wife and raise a crop, and if the Yankees fool with me any more, I'll whip 'em again."[1]

---

[1] Harris 1890, 83. Among the members of the audience was the former Union General William T. Sherman, whom Grady acknowledged, saying, "...he is kind of a careless man about fire...." This statement immediately followed the reference to Sandersville, which had been one of Sherman's temporary headquarters on his March to the Sea, and where he had burned the town's entire commercial district and courthouse, sparing only the local Masonic Hall. It is likely that only Sherman would have immediately recognized the meaning of this reference.

Between Grady's espoused vision and the quoted plans of the mythical veteran, the latter was far closer to the truth. Despite the relatively modest growth of cities like Atlanta, Macon, Savannah, and Columbus, Georgia remained a state whose population was diffused throughout a myriad of small towns and country crossroads and whose prime source of livelihood was agriculture, mainly cotton. Beyond the neo-sophistication of the state's few cities, the vast majority of the population lived in muddy hamlets separated from one another by often-impassable dirt tracks, pursuing a lifestyle not appreciably changed from that of the Roman Empire some two millennia earlier.

The years following the Civil War were not good ones for Georgia. The Confederacy's economic gambit to lure European support by the threat of the loss of its major cotton source had failed. In addition to the warehouses, farm equipment, and railroads, the slave-dependent system that formed the basis of the agricultural economy had been destroyed. The major centers of American cotton production had now moved to newer lands in the west, as the worn-out soils that had so richly rewarded plantation owners a few decades earlier produced less and less.

Amid the gloom there were some bright spots. In Hancock County, David Dickson—"The Prince of Southern Farmers"— was once again profitably farming thousands of acres of cotton. He had achieved near-legendary fame practicing "scientific farming" while increasing his holdings from a mere 266 acres and a few slaves in 1845 to 13,000 acres and 250 slaves at the start of the war.[2] The vast majority of farmers, however, struggled to eke out a profitable existence, beset by unpredictable fluctuations in price, uncertain labor practices, uncooperative

---

[2] Range 1954, 22.

weather, and periodic "panics" that plunged many into bankruptcy. From an agricultural standpoint, one historian described the period between the end of the Civil War and the turn of the century as "The Long Depression."[3]

The post-war period in Georgia was in many ways a living experiment in social evolution. After the plantation system died, new ways of harnessing labor were needed. With a limited banking system, some means of financing crops that were harvested once a year had to be found. The trends that evolved were to set the state's course for the next half-century or more. Among the many practices to emerge from the ashes of war were the tenant farming system, the continued dominance of cotton as the primary crop, and non-cash barter and credit practices. While these sustained the agricultural economy, they planted the seeds of its eventual collapse decades later.

In 1860, 90 percent of the African-American population of the United States was confined to the South. By 1900, this percentage was essentially unchanged. For all their ardor in freeing the slaves, people in the North had no great eagerness to accept them as free citizens. Impediments to migration, both overt and subtle, were common. The South, meanwhile, was faced with hundreds of thousands of unemployed blacks who were uncertain of their place in society and unversed in the marketplace of commerce. During the formal period of Reconstruction, the Freedmen's Bureau and other groups tried to establish systems of contract wage labor, most of which failed miserably. Landowners, including former plantation owners and those who had snapped up farms at depressed prices after the war, had fields that needed to be planted and tilled. Former slaves and returning war veterans alike needed a

---

[3] Ibid., 75.

way to make a living and earn sustenance for their families. A system of tenant farming developed that—while imperfect—offered some degree of satisfaction to both groups.

The term "tenant farming" is broadly used to describe the relationship between a landowner and a person who, for some sort of payment, agrees to tend the land. There was no universal standard across the South. Most agreements followed local habits and were highly variable depending on the quality and location of the land, among other factors. In the most simple form, a tenant farmer would pay a landowner for the use of his property to grow crops. Payments could be made in currency, but many were made in products harvested from the land. This practice lasted well into the twentieth century. In 1908, for example, a 200-acre Washington County farm was advertised as being for rent for 8 bales of cotton per year.[4]

A more common arrangement, and one that came to be preferred by both landowner and tenant alike, was referred to as sharecropping. The theory behind this relationship allowed both the landowner and the tenant to share the risks and the rewards. Practices were local and empiric, but a common arrangement was based on "thirds." Using the land as one third, the labor as another third, and the cost of crop production as the final third, the owner and 'cropper would each share in the harvest based on his contribution. For example, if the tenant furnished only his labor, and the landowner furnished the land, a house, and the cost of planting and harvesting, at the end of the crop year the tenant would be due one-third and the landowner the rest. In reality, it rarely worked this way.

The landowner often took advantage of the tenant, advancing him money or provisions to be deducted from his

---

[4] Jordan 1989.

share of the division at the end of the crop year. Many tenants ended up with little to show other than a year's hard labor and debts to be carried forward against the next crop. Tenants, on the other hand, had little incentive to take care of the land. Erosion was common, and by the early twentieth century the agricultural landscape was scarred by gullies slicing into poorly maintained fields.

For all the good and bad of the tenant farming system, the practice grew with time. In 1880, the first year that the United States Census recorded the type of farm operation, some 44.9 percent of farms were operated by tenants.[5] By 1900, this figure had grown to 59.9 percent, and it jumped to 65.6 percent in 1910 when nearly two-thirds of all Georgia workers were directly employed in agriculture. The racial disparity was striking. In 1910, for example, 50 percent of white farmers were tenants, while the figure was 87 percent for those classed as "colored."[6]

Even prior to the Civil War, many recognized the inherent weakness of an agricultural economy based on a single crop. As was often pointed out by agronomists and economists alike, the South's focus on cotton production increased the cost of everything else. In the absence of a broader commercial and industrial base, necessities from plow lines to plows and the mules to pull them had to be brought in from elsewhere, increasing the cost of production and cutting into profits. Despite this, the worn catchphrase of "Cotton is King" remained the order of the day.

During the Civil War, cotton prices had soared, as would any commodity whose supply is threatened, and they remained high in the immediate post-war period. The states of

---

[5] Range 1954.
[6] United States Census 1910.

the former Confederacy were now under the administration of military and Federal government bureaucrats who often were no less eager than the former plantation owners to cash in on cotton's fabled riches. Even Harriet Beecher Stowe, whose book *Uncle Tom's Cabin* had so inflamed anti-slavery forces worldwide, could not resist the lure of cotton. Writing some years later in *The Atlantic*, she recounted how she and her family members had rented a 9,000-acre plantation in Florida just after the war, living in the decaying splendor of the main house and hiring former slaves to till the fields. In justifying this, her "process of reasoning was very simple: *cotton* is the one thing *sure* always to be wanted in the world."[7]

Indeed, cotton was the "one thing." Unlike conventional food crops or animals, it didn't get sick, it didn't spoil or die, it could be warehoused until the market price was right, and 500-pound bales were hard to steal. With a steady domestic and international demand, it became in effect a form of currency, something that could be sold, bartered, or traded for future credit. Furthermore, the system to grow it was already in place. Georgia's vast fields once again turned white each autumn, filled with rows of men, women, and children dragging long sacks that bulged with cotton destined for mills in Europe and the Northeast.

On a practical basis, rural Georgia in the latter part of the nineteenth century became a near-cashless society. This is not to imply that the majority of commercial transactions were not eventually settled with currency, but for those two-thirds of workers who were directly engaged in agriculture, significant quantities of cash were available only after the harvest was sold. What would have been considered routine forms of credit in the latter half of the twentieth century were simply not

---

[7] Stowe 1879. Italics are those of Stowe.

available. Land, *per se*, both plentiful and taxed as the main source of local income, was a near-valueless liability unless it could be made productive. Banks were few in number and loosely regulated. While bankers might be willing to loan on a tangible asset such as bales of cotton in a warehouse, advancing money against a crop yet to be harvested was considered risky speculation.

Georgia's first crop lien law was enacted in 1866 in the post-war period.[8] In the ensuing years, this became the main source of credit for farmers and the mainstay of economic life in Georgia's small towns. The North was often the ultimate source of the funds that circulated in the South. Banks, wholesalers, and brokers would extend credit to landowners and merchants. They in turn would loan to farmers, many of whom were tenants. Often the merchant would assume the role of banker, extending credit in exchange for a lien on an unharvested crop. Other times the landowner, himself a borrower, would re-extend credit to his tenants. In all cases, the markup was significant. Merchants not only factored in an appreciable profit but also subjected goods charged on credit to interest rates as high as 75 to 100 percent per annum.

Such exorbitant rates may have smacked of usury, but the risks were significant. As a creditor, the merchant's security was a crop whose ultimate value was subject to the uncertainties of weather, insects, and a final price that would be set months hence. The ability of the farmer to pay was uncertain at best, and in bad crop years such loans were often subject to default.

Based on the logistical and financial constraints of the system, life in rural Georgia settled into a rhythm. Small market towns, surrounded by smaller villages, functioned as

---

[8] Coleman 1991, 227.

independent economic units within the larger economy. In 1900, only 15.7 percent of Georgia's 2.2 million citizens lived in towns larger than 2,500, and only 6 towns in the state had a population of greater than 10,000.[9] For much of the year, many farmers came to town once a week, often on Saturday, to buy staples or catch up on the local news and gossip.

While county newspapers advertised farm equipment, animals, and services year-round, their pages filled with advertisements for consumer goods as the harvest season progressed and people were able to pay with cash. Fall was the time for county fairs as the cotton was "laid by" in the weeks between the final hoeing and harvest. Georgia counties' inconvenient deadline for the payment of property taxes in December is a residual of the irregular agricultural cash flows of the nineteenth century. As the cotton crop poured in, commercial gin operations along the many "Cotton Avenues" often ran late into the night. Mule-drawn wagons lined up at first light, as farmers waited patiently, chewing tobacco and swapping stories. Warehouses overflowed, and tightly packed quarter-ton bales of cotton lined the streets, awaiting transport to the seaports and their final destinations.

Considered from an agricultural standpoint, the nineteenth century ended with a whimper. The Panic of 1893 took its toll on farmers with the plunge in cotton prices leading to bankruptcy for more than a few. By 1900, the total value of Georgia's annual agricultural production had declined significantly when compared to 1870.[10] An average farm in the state, including implements and stock, was worth some 45 percent below its value a few years after the war.[11]

---

[9] Range 1954, 99.

[10] Ibid., 151.

[11] Ibid.

But all was not gloom. If Grady's vision of the New South was more dream than reality in the mid-1880s, positive change was underway. The spinning and weaving industry of the Northeast had begun to migrate south, offering other alternatives for employment. Short-line railroads were organized to connect Georgia's far-flung fields to the main stream of commerce. The cry for economic diversification was being heeded, with increasing growth of alternative crops. In south Georgia, the timber and turpentine industries were expanding. Even for those who continued to grow cotton, per-acre yields were increasing due to more careful selection of seed variety and more sophisticated use of fertilizer. The new century would see a veritable explosion in the number of Georgia's banks, relieving to a degree the onerous nature of credit. Taken together, these trends would usher in a period of unrivaled agricultural prosperity, a Golden Age of small towns.

5

Movers and Shakers

From the perspective of the early twenty-first century, Georgia's small towns might seem to be vestiges of a dead-end branch on the tree of social evolution. In contrast to the gleaming bustle of the city, they lie stagnant, their populations older, poorer, and less educated. They are often found in what appear to be incongruously out-of-the-way places, as if their first settlers were seeking solitude or the chance to form a new social order unfettered by the constraints of the past. The truth is far more prosaic.

In America, as in the rest of the world, the sites of settlements that later became towns and cities were chosen for reasons that have little to do with their current existence. For example, Philadelphia and Baltimore, as well as Richmond, Virginia, and Columbia, South Carolina, are known as "Fall Line cities" for their location on the geologic transition between the rocky and rolling granite hills of the Piedmont and the sedimentary Coastal Plain. Their sites represented the highest point of unimpeded navigation on their respective rivers, a place where goods had to be unloaded from boats or barges and transferred to wagons for the further journey inland. In Georgia, the settlements that became Augusta, Milledgeville, Macon, and Columbus are Fall Line cities[1] as well; today these cities are no longer dependent on river traffic.

---

[1]There were others, also, including the lost city of Georgetown just below the "great falls" of Ogeechee, reputedly named for King George III.

The pattern of scattered settlement as it developed in Georgia throughout the nineteenth century was based on agriculture, and for much of the state, this meant cotton. With variations and exceptions, cotton was the primary crop in the middle to lower Piedmont and in the upper and middle Coastal Plain. Mountainous areas in the north and northwest of the state and the low-lying sections of the southeast were less intensively farmed. With some regularity, larger towns are found about thirty miles apart, a good day's journey by horse-drawn coach. In between were smaller settlements where horses could be fed and watered, food could be had for travelers, and perhaps lodging found for the night.

As the century evolved and the population increased, country crossroads became the social and business focus of local areas. There might be a simple country store with the basic provisions for farm and home, a blacksmith shop, and perhaps a gin and limited warehouse space. These services were often provided by farmers or landowners, with many—perhaps most—of their customers being tenant farmers who bought their goods on credit.

By the last quarter of the century, the pattern was well established. A central market town—commonly the county seat—would be surrounded by a constellation of smaller villages, which in turn would have their own satellite network of crossroads stores providing the most basic goods and services. The central towns were usually served by rail, which brought in the heavier goods and took away commodities. The short-line railroads that connected to the main lines commonly had small sidings or depots every few miles to facilitate delivery of bulk supplies such as fertilizer, and to pick up bales of cotton or other heavy goods destined for more distant markets.

Historians often speak of social and economic change as if it occurs spontaneously, leading to outcomes that should have seemed obvious even from the perspective of the era. While this might have validity on a larger scale, events in Georgia's small towns of the nineteenth and early twentieth centuries can often be traced to a few individuals who, for whatever reason, had the means and ability to make things happen. Occasionally, the motivation might have been altruistic; more commonly it was simple American entrepreneurship, the ethic of hard work coupled with a personal desire for economic gain. If the community happened to benefit, then all the better. From that class of citizens whose resources and desires allowed something beyond mere survival of self and family came the merchants, the bankers, the investors in railroads and warehouses, and, in turn, progress.

Almost every county seat had its first families, those who had been among the early settlers and who had managed to accumulate enough wealth and power to assure their place in the economic and social history of the community. Some prospered and failed. Others left a legacy that lasted for generations. For Charlie Rawlings and his cousin, Gus Tarbutton, it should have been the latter. They were typical of the breed of men who thrived in small towns at the turn of the century. Indeed, for decades, both men seemed to lead a charmed life until the fates turned against them.

While the two cousins' legacies were permanently tinted by the events of 1925, their earlier lives were in some ways remarkably similar. Both were hard workers and shrewd businessmen. Both sought their fortunes in agriculture—Gus as a farmer, Charlie as a livery stable operator who expanded into farming, banking, and other investments. Both shared similar family tragedies. Each was involved in a conflict that resulted in the violent death of a brother. While in the end neither suffered direct consequences of these misfortunes, they became part of the public persona of each man.

By the1890s, Charlie was well on the road to success. His businesses were thriving. He was well connected politically. His sister was the wife of Sandersville's mayor, and his own wife's second cousin, Maude, was married to Tom Hardwick, his brother's law partner and a man who would later figure greatly in the lives of both Charlie and his cousin Gus. In 1893, Charlie had been one of the founders of the Sandersville Railroad, profitable despite boasting of only four miles of standard-gauge track, one locomotive, and one passenger car.

In 1898, Charlie and his brother, together with Tom Hardwick and five Perkins brothers and cousins related to Charlie's wife, incorporated the Reidsville & Dorchester Railroad, a proposed fifty-mile-line connecting the agricultural center of Reidsville to the seacoast in Liberty County.[2] Meanwhile, Charlie was quietly purchasing cropland and expanding his businesses to supply farmers not only with horses and mules but also with seed and fertilizer. Often in partnership with other local businessmen, he acquired gins and warehouses in surrounding counties.

In the rough-and-tumble world of small-town commerce at the turn of the century, Charlie Rawlings was an aggressive player. The fine details of his business life may have been lost, but the written record reveals a man whose ethics were flexible to say the least, and for whom defeat simply meant a chance to regroup and try again. He made aggressive and frequent use of the court system, sometimes losing but never hesitant to pursue his side of the case, right or wrong. In the three decades between 1892 and 1922, at least seven cases in which Charlie

---

[2] The coastal railroad project was apparently never completed.

Rawlings was a plaintiff or defendant made their way to the Georgia Court of Appeals or state Supreme Court for final adjudication.[3] Two are illustrative of his personality.

The furnishing of money for bail bonds is a profitable if somewhat seedy business. In spring 1913, Charlie Rawlings had signed a bond for one Tom Tompkins, who was charged with a criminal offense in nearby Jefferson County. When the defendant failed to appear in court, a judgment was issued against Charlie for the relatively trivial amount of $150. The sheriff of Washington County, B. A. English, served him with notice of his debt to the court for that amount, plus interest. Charlie objected, stating that he had never been served with the legal documents, despite the fact that the sheriff filed an affidavit that he had done so.

As was his custom, Charlie hired Tom Hardwick, and they began an aggressive defense of his position. In addition to swearing that he'd not been served, he attacked the entire legality of the process, amending his suit to include the sheriff and stating that he should have "his day in court" before a judgment could be rendered and the defaulted bond collected. The justices ruled against him. The costs of his legal challenge[4] no doubt vastly exceeded the amount he otherwise would have paid by simply accepting the fact that Tom Tompkins had failed to appear in court.

Another case[5] that came before the state Supreme Court opens a window on Charlie Rawlings's sense of morality, or perhaps lack thereof. In early 1908, three siblings, Isabella Brooks, Ella Nora Brooks, and Leon Brooks appealed, to him

---

[3] The events of 1925 resulted in a number of additional appeals through the state court system, but these come later in the tale.

[4] *Rawlings v. Brown*, 15 Ga.App. 162, 82 S.E. 803 (1914).

[5] *Brooks v. Rawlings*, 1912.

for a loan to be secured by some property they had inherited. They were in debt, unable to pay, and were being sued by their creditors. Faced with the prospect of losing their farms, they appealed to Charlie for a loan to satisfy their creditors and salvage their inheritance. He readily agreed, offering to take over management of the land, leasing it out, collecting the rent, and applying it to their indebtedness until the note was paid. The one stipulation was that he would need "an absolute deed" to the property, because without it, he said he would not have the necessary authority to manage it.

According to court documents, Charlie "professed great friendship for the [siblings] on account of his friendship for their father, and said that he would treat them fairly and properly in the matter." They accepted his proposal, relying on him to prepare the necessary papers. But, as the court would later state, "they were unlearned in legal matters, and acted without the advice of counsel or others skilled in such matters." At the time, the land was said to be worth $3,000, a princely sum when farms were selling for a few dollars an acre. The siblings received $972.92 from Charlie to pay their debts. He in turn collected at least $1,400 income from the property over the next three years.

The Brookses eventually received word that Charlie Rawlings was saying that he had bought the land from them in a fair transaction, that he owned it free and clear, and that they had no interest in it whatsoever. They offered to pay him back whatever they owed him, but he refused. They sued in the Superior Court of Washington County. With Hardwick as Rawlings's defense counsel, their case against him was dismissed. The matter reached the state Supreme Court in spring 1912. The Court unanimously ruled against Rawlings, stating that "he procured [the] deed fraudulently, by taking advantage of [the Brookses'] ignorance and of the confidence reposed in him by them." The case stayed in the courts for more than a decade, eventually returning to the Supreme Court in 1921.[6] Among the several attorneys representing the Brooks family was R. Earl Camp of Dublin, a man who some years later would sit in judgment over Charlie Rawlings.

Though he was chastised, it appears unlikely that this defeat caused Charlie to pause for moral reflection. His reputation was well known, and his propensity for aggressive use of the legal system would not change. Perhaps he was unaware, or perhaps he simply didn't care about the collateral damage his actions were capable of inflicting on others. Clearly, the events of nearly twenty years earlier that led to his brother's death seemed not to have taught him a lesson.

---

[6] *Brooks v. Rawlings*, 152 Ga.394 110 S.E. 159 (1921).

Unintended Consequences

Shortly after two o'clock on the sunny Saturday afternoon of July 15, 1893, Fred Rawlings and Richard Roughton shot and killed each other under the shade of a mulberry tree in the middle of Sandersville's crowded City Square. The series of events that led to the killings was complex and convoluted, involving two prominent and related families, a land dispute, a legal decision by the Georgia Supreme Court, the temperance movement, and a blind tiger. Beyond the tragedy, the killings would help shape the reputation of Charlie Rawlings.

In almost every oft-repeated tale emerging from small-town Georgia of the 1890s, complicated family, business, and personal relationships have a prominent role. The so-called Rawlings-Roughton Shootout was no exception. By 1890, Charlie Rawlings was a rising star in Sandersville's small-business community. His livery stable was profitable, and he was well connected politically. He had served several terms on the City Council, and his sister, Lavinia, was married to Bradford E. Roughton, Sandersville's mayor and a member of another prominent family.

In March of that year, several well-located residential lots came up for sale near the City Square. They had been owned by a widow named Pittman and were to be sold at public auction. There were two lots facing South Harris Street, a corner lot that Charlie wanted as a site on which to build his home, and a second lot next door that bordered the residence of his brother-in-law, the mayor. Roughton was willing to let

Charlie buy the property on the corner, but both men wanted ownership of the lot between them. After discussing the matter, they agreed that rather than start a bidding war, one of them would purchase the middle lot at the auction, afterward sharing the cost equally and dividing the property down the middle. Roughton agreed to do the bidding and bought the lot for $395. Both men were present at the sale.

After the auction, Charlie approached the auctioneer and asked that the deed be made jointly in his name and that of Roughton. The man refused, stating that he'd sold it to Roughton, not to both men. The parties agreed, and the lot was put in Roughton's name with the plan that a new deed would be prepared later. The next day, when Charlie approached his brother-in-law to pay his half of the cost, he was told there was a new condition—his half of the property would not be delivered until he had taken up residence on the corner lot he had just purchased.

Charlie brought suit against Bradford Roughton, alleging fraud and breach of contract. The agreement was entirely an oral one, and while Roughton did not dispute his brother-in-law's allegations, he pointed out that such an agreement was not considered a valid contract and was therefore unenforceable. The lower courts found in his favor, but the case was appealed to Georgia's Supreme Court. On October 1, 1892, the justices held that Roughton was correct and confirmed his valid title to the disputed property. If the matter had ended there, it likely would have meant little more than injured egos and awkward family gatherings. But it did not, and ill will between the two families quietly festered beneath the commerce of everyday life.

By the last decade of the nineteenth century, the sale of liquor had long been illegal in the city of Sandersville. This had been the goal of the Friends of Temperance, the Woman's Christian Temperance Union, and other similar groups with the common dream of the total elimination of "demon rum." Prominent among the leaders of the temperance movement was Bradford Roughton, the mayor. The men of the Rawlings family, on the other hand, clearly had little use for the concept, especially if it interfered with their ability to make money on the side.

The prohibition law was widely ignored, especially around election time. Liquor by the bottle or drink was easily obtained, and more than a few of the stores surrounding the City Square had basements that served as makeshift saloons. These were referred to as "blind tigers," the southern equivalent of the better-known term "speakeasy."

It was a complex tale. On Friday, July 14, 1893, Arch Jones, a barber, testified in the Mayor's Court that he had purchased whiskey from Taylor Birdsong, a porter and drayman at the grocery store on the City Square owned and operated by John Rawlings, a cousin of Charlie Rawlings and his sister Lavinia, Mayor Roughton's wife. The mayor, having recused himself because of his relationship to the Rawlings family, had the mayor issue pro tem an arrest warrant for John Rawlings. At a court hearing the following morning, Fred Rawlings, Charlie's and Lavinia's brother, was present in support of his cousin, John. He was overheard making disparaging remarks about the prohibitionist mayor, apparently referring to Roughton's recent legal dispute with Charlie.

These comments reached the ear of Richard Roughton, the mayor's brother, who set out in search of Fred Rawlings. As far as anyone knew, the two men were friends. Any hard feelings between their brothers had not changed that. Finding Fred at his cousin's store, Richard called him outside to talk. They were observed standing under the mulberry tree near Dr. William Rawlings's drugstore. Without warning, a volley of shots rang out, followed by a pause, then more shots. Within seconds, both men were on the ground, struggling, and were quickly surrounded by businessmen, shop owners, and passersby from the square.

The two wounded men were carried into the nearby drugstore. Roughton, dripping blood on the wood flooring from three bullet wounds to his left temple, died shortly thereafter without regaining consciousness. Fred Rawlings, pale from shock and two gunshot wounds in his abdomen just below his heart, was told of Roughton's death. He said he wanted to die, too, and did within thirty minutes. His brother Charlie was at his side.

Immediately after the shootings, rumors spread that a "third person," unnamed in the newspaper reports, had fired on Roughton after he had fallen. Charlie Rawlings had been observed standing beside the fallen men with a gun in his hand, but he was said to have "picked up one of the pistols that had fallen from the grasp of one of the principals in the tragedy." John Rawlings and another cousin were there also. All three men were arrested, the latter two held at the jail and Charlie kept under guard at his residence, a courtesy warranted by his place of prominence in the community. A coroner's jury was assembled and viewed the bodies. A hearing was scheduled for the following Monday, July 17, to hear testimony on the killings.

The hearing took place in a courtroom crowded with spectators, the deaths of two prominent young men attracting the curiosity of a town morbidly eager to hear firsthand the exact sequence of events. There was no shortage of eyewitnesses. The shootings had occurred in the most public spot in the county in the high afternoon of the busiest day of the week. The accounts varied widely, perhaps—as one news report suggested—influenced by relationship or friendship with the dead men or their families. A total of twenty-four witnesses—fewer than those who had actually been called— were examined before the coroner's jury decided they had heard enough.

Estimates of the number of shots fired ranged from four to thirteen. The consensus seemed to be that Charlie Rawlings was the first on the scene, having rushed over from his nearby livery stable office. Once the shooting started, both John Rawlings and another cousin were seen with their pistols drawn, but no one reported that they had fired a shot. The real issue seemed to be Charlie Rawlings's degree of involvement in the scuffle between the two doomed men. He had been observed with a pistol in his hand, and one witness said he had seen him fire it. Another thought he had seen Charlie with a knife, and a third—who had also approached the scene with his pistol drawn—testified that Charlie had lunged at him with his gun. Several said that they thought he had come to the aid of his brother, but in the end, the jury drew the conclusion that Charlie was only trying to separate the men. In a pointed exoneration, the jury found "that Charles G. Rawlings only acted as a peacemaker." Despite their drawn weapons, John Rawlings and the cousin were found to have "had nothing to do with the killing."

Fred Rawlings was buried in the family plot in the city's Old Cemetery, where his brother Charlie would join him nearly half a century later. Though Charlie was absolved of any involvement in the killings, doubts lingered in the minds of some, perhaps reinforced by the testimony given to the coroner's jury. Despite the tragedy, life went on, and Charlie's wealth grew with the passing years. As for the mayor, a brief paragraph in the *Sandersville Herald* ten days after the killing reminded voters that he would not be running for reelection and suggested that a committee be formed to nominate a new candidate. He and Lavinia moved away shortly thereafter, never again to live in their hometown.

7

The Uncertain Line Between Truth and Justice

While Charlie Rawlings led a very public life, less is known about Gus Tarbutton's earlier years. Despite the difference in their ages, he and Charlie were known to be close. Charlie was said to have introduced Gus to his future wife, and he was a frequent social companion. He had helped Gus and his older brother Herschel get started as farmers, advising them and providing financial support as needed.

The end of the cotton season of 1906 found the Tarbutton brothers, Herschel and Gus, residing in the western part of Johnson County near the scattered settlement known as the Buckeye community. They had established themselves as successful farmers, running perhaps the largest operation in the county. In May of that year, Gus Tarbutton purchased a 600-acre tract of land in Laurens County near the Johnson County line. It was adjacent to land he already owned and contained some merchantable timber. Moreover, he was likely able to obtain it at a good price. The original owner had moved to south Georgia and had recently repossessed the property from a previous buyer who was in default on his note payments. Or such was Tarbutton's understanding.

The tract had been owned by a man named Young whose plan was to purchase other property with the proceeds of the sale of his land in Laurens County. He had first sold it to Letcher Tyre, described as a "prominent timber and sawmill operator" from the Dublin area. As it was nearly impossible to obtain financing through banks, Young followed the then-standard practice of taking a down payment and issuing a title to Tyre based on his receipt of periodic payments until the debt was retired. By early 1906, Tyre had fallen behind on the payments on which Young relied to meet his financial obligations in his new location. He declared Tyre's provisional title void, and he resold the land to Gus Tarbutton.

A few days after acquiring the property, Tarbutton heard the sound of chopping in the woods. He investigated and found three men cutting timber "for Mr. Letcher Tyre." He wrote a note to Tyre, who replied that he still had possession of the land, and it was his right to cut his own timber. Tarbutton responded by swearing out warrants for the laborers. When the matter came up in court, the case was deferred to the November session. Tyre was not pleased.

On Friday, November 9, 1906, word reached Tarbutton that Tyre was setting up a sawmill on the disputed property, apparently intending to cut timber to which he still claimed title. Summoning his brother Herschel and his brother-in-law, Joe Fluker, the three men rode out on horseback to confront Tyre and his crew. They arrived to find a sawmill operation, but Tyre was off in the nearby swamp hunting squirrels. He was sent for and greeted the three horsemen with, "What will you have, gentlemen?" He was still holding the breech-loading shotgun near his chest.

The exact sequence of events that followed varies depending on whether the account came from those who witnessed the confrontation or from those who participated in it. Within a matter of moments of the men's arrival in the clearing, Letcher Tyre lay mortally injured from a gunshot wound to his abdomen, while Herschel Tarbutton had received a blast of shotgun pellets to his head that would prove fatal two days later. It was generally agreed that Herschel had fired the fatal bullet that would kill Tyre, who had fired the blast that would result in Herschel's death. The only dispute seemed to be who fired first.

With his brother gravely wounded, Gus commandeered Tyre's horse and buggy, setting off toward Sandersville and their cousin's hospital, hoping to save Herschel's life. Tyre was left to fend for himself. With assistance from his men, he managed to walk a quarter mile to the home of a neighbor, where he died about midnight the same day. Meanwhile, Herschel was in the Rawlings Sanitarium in Sandersville under the care of his first cousin, Dr. William Rawlings.[1] He died near midday on Sunday, two days later. Both men made dying declarations that the other had fired first.

A fatal shootout between members of two prominent families earned front-page headlines in the local papers the following week. The *Sandersville Herald* was quick to take the side of the Tarbuttons, commenting that "the physical facts and circumstances seem to corroborate" their versions, even before the evidence had been presented in court. The *Wrightsville Chronicle* noted, "The Tarbutton family is one of the most prominent of Washington County," but tempered its praise by observing, "While successful and good business men, they attended strictly to their own business and lived very closely upon their places, and hence have never been as popular as they otherwise might have been, though they have some very close friends."[2] Close friends or not, it was going to take more than community support to save Gus Tarbutton and Joe Fluker from a charge of premeditated murder.

---

[1] The author's great-uncle.

[2] For information on the regional newspapers consulted for this work, see "Sources and Context" below.

Gus was arrested in Sandersville on Sunday afternoon following his brother's death. Joe Fluker surrendered shortly thereafter. Both men were taken to the jail in Dublin, where they were held without bail pending a hearing. Their initial court appearance was postponed for a week while both sides assembled legal teams. In Laurens County, feelings were running strongly against the men accused of killing a local citizen, and rumors began to spread that Herschel Tarbutton was in fact not dead and that a dummy had been buried in his place. It was said that he had been spirited away to avoid facing a murder charge of which he was surely guilty.

On November 16, a week after the shootings, Tarbutton and Fluker were brought before a judge for their preliminary hearing. "A large crowd," many of them Tarbutton supporters from Johnson and Washington counties, was present to witness the spectacle. An affidavit attesting to the fact that Herschel Tarbutton was indeed dead and buried was presented from the Sandersville chief of police. The presiding judge was quickly disqualified, having "previously…expressed an opinion as to what he intended to do in the cases." A second hearing was scheduled for a week later. The men remained in jail.

Meanwhile, a legal defense team was being assembled, co-ordinated, and funded by the deep pockets of Gus's first cousin and mentor, Charlie Rawlings. The lead counsel for the defense was to be Charlie's friend and personal attorney, Thomas W. Hardwick, the dynamic young congressman from Georgia's Tenth District, in addition to other prominent attorneys from Wrightsville, Sandersville, and Dublin. Not to be outmaneu-vered, the state retained the firm of the fiery former congress-man, Thomas E. Watson, to assist in the prosecution.

On Friday, November 23, the parties once again convened in a Dublin courtroom for the preliminary hearing. This time a panel of three justices of the peace had been assembled to hear the case. The *Dublin Courier-Dispatch*, ever supportive of local causes, reported the events under a front-page headline that read, "Tyre Begged Not to Be Shot." Meanwhile, the *Sandersville Herald* limited its reporting to Gus Tarbutton's and Joe Fluker's statements, which painted the events in an entirely different light.

The prosecution's first witness was Dr. William R. Brigham, the physician who had attended to Letcher Tyre in his final hours. He testified that Tyre had been killed by a single shot to the abdomen. On cross-examination, he opined that the bullet seemed to have been fired from an elevated position, which would have been the case if the shooter were on horseback.

The next and only witness to testify about the details of the killings was one of Tyre's employees, Bill Johnson. Described as "a negro about grown," he testified that after a brief exchange of words, Herschel had drawn his pistol and shot first at Tyre, who returned fire, striking Tarbutton in the head. Following these initial shots, Johnson said Gus Tarbutton and Joe Fluker drew their pistols and also fired at Tyre. He stated that all of the men remained on their horses during the melee. The defense scored points on cross-examination when Johnson was unable to correctly identify Tarbutton and Fluker in the courtroom.

Lee Woodrum and another negro who had been present at the shooting and scheduled to testify for the prosecution could not be found. Johnson said they had disappeared in the company of some companions who had offered them "$25 or $30" to testify for the side of the defendants. Hardwick objected, stating that it could not be proven that the defendants had anything to do with the attempt to purchase the witnesses' testimony. The court agreed, and that portion of Johnson's testimony was thrown out.

Although it seemed to be generally agreed that the shootings took place in Laurens County, a witness who had lived in the area for forty years was called to confirm this. On cross-examination by the defense, he admitted that his only source of information as to the exact location of the county line was what he had always been told. A back-up defense strategy contesting jurisdiction was beginning to emerge.

Finally, J. B. Tyre, Letcher's brother, testified that the dying man remained conscious until a few minutes before his death, and that he said Herschel Tarbutton had fired at him first.

The defense presented testimony from Gus Tarbutton and Joe Fluker. Both stated that Tyre started the shooting, firing first at Gus Tarbutton but missing and hitting his horse, then firing the fatal blast that killed Herschel. Gus was careful to explain that he had dismounted from his horse and was having a smoke when Tyre fired at him. After the shooting, they testified that they offered help to the wounded Tyre, assuring themselves of his welfare before departing to Sandersville with Herschel.

The ruling by the justice of the peace held that there was reasonable cause to detain Tarbutton and Fluker on a charge of murder. The following Monday, November 26, Hardwick convinced a Superior Court judge to grant them bail in the amount of $20,000 each, presenting statements from physicians that confinement in the common jail would permanently impair their health. In January, a Laurens County grand jury formally indicted them for murder. A jury trial was scheduled to take place during the next term of court later that month.

In its January 30, 1907 issue, the *Wrightsville Chronicle* set the stage for a major courtroom battle: "It is predicted that the trial will result in the hardest fought trials that have ever occurred in this section of Georgia.... The defendants belong to some of the most prominent families in this part of the state, and are highly connected, being people of prominence and property." The article also mentioned "that the county line between Laurens and Johnson is to play an important feature in the trial."

The long-awaited trial ended almost as soon as it had begun. The defense announced that it had a sworn affidavit from a witness present when Herschel Tarbutton gave his dying declaration. This witness, a court reporter, was prepared to swear that Tarbutton stated in his final words that he alone had shot and killed Tyre, thus absolving his brother and Joe Fluker of any guilt. Unfortunately, the witness had recently undergone an operation for appendicitis and was unable to appear. Furthermore, Lee Woodrum, "an important eye-witness" to the affray, "could not be found." Several other key witnesses sent affidavits from physicians attesting to their ill health.

Tom Hardwick, the lead defense counsel, told the judge that as a congressman and member of the Rivers and Harbors Committee, he needed to be present in Washington, DC, to make an important vote on a bill that would mean "a large appropriation" for the district. A trial at the time would prevent him from going. A. F. Daley, the second-ranking defense counsel, complained of "a very severe cold," making it impossible for him to continue in court for even the remainder of the day.

The presiding judge called Gus Tarbutton to the stand to question him on several issues regarding trial procedure. Gus admitted that C. G. Rawlings had employed most of the counsel for the defense. When asked about the absence of Woodrum, the eyewitness, he replied that he had not seen him since the preceding December. The court bailiff countered that he had been in Sandersville a few days earlier and had seen the missing Woodrum at Rawlings's stables, describing him distinctively as "a medium sized yellow negro with a glass eye." When the bailiff returned with orders from the Laurens County sheriff to take the man into custody, Woodrum could not be found. The judge reluctantly granted a continuance until the July term of court.

Three days later, the front page of the *Courier-Dispatch* displayed the bold headline, "Highly Sensational Was the Petition." As the judge who had granted the continuance was preparing to adjourn for the term, he was presented with "a most unusual and very novel petition." It was signed by J. B. Tyre, brother of the dead man and prosecutor of the case against Tarbutton and Fluker. In it, Tyre alleged that Lee Woodrum, the missing eyewitness, was "in the custody and control of said defendants or their friends," and could have been made to appear "had the defendants desired to go to trial." He further alleged that the defendants had "summoned some fifty odd witnesses" and would attempt to find excuses to continue the case from term to term until such time as it would be effectively dropped, "thereby delaying justice and defeating the law."

Tyre continued that he believed the defendants were "guilty of willful murder, a diabolical assassination, going to the place of business of the said J. L. Tyre, armed to the teeth, and shooting him to death while he was begging for his life." He requested that the court revoke the bail of Tarbutton and Fluker, and that they be examined by "five impartial physicians" to determine if in fact confinement in jail would be dangerous for their health. The court took the petition under advisement. The defendants remained free on bail.

For whatever success the defense had achieved thus far in helping Tarbutton and Fluker avoid a jury, the long-term outlook was not good. The facts—if the witnesses could be found—appeared to be against them, and furthermore, the trial was to take place in a county where public sentiment made conviction more likely. Even if they were able to avoid a charge of premeditated murder, a lesser finding of accessory to murder could result in lengthy prison sentences. There had been talk of requesting a change of venue, but another and more permanent solution to the problem presented itself.

Johnson County was formed in 1858 by an act of the Georgia Legislature, its area carved from the adjacent counties of Washington, Laurens, and Emanuel. On its western border, the new county claimed about three and a half miles of river frontage on the Oconee River. The southern county line defining the border with Laurens County began on the east side of the river, "opposite the mouth of Big Sandy Creek," then proceeded in an easterly direction for approximately five and a half miles before turning south. The point where the line changed direction was defined as "the ford of Forts Creek where the Sandersville and Dublin road crosses the same." Both end points were unmarked, and their exact locations were imprecise at best.

A formal survey had been made when the county was formed, done by a Mr. James Hicks, described as "a man of considerable intelligence, and a Surveyor of some note in his section." In the half century that had elapsed since the original survey, both counties had collected taxes and maintained the roads on their respective sides of the established line.

Apparently in response to a request from Hardwick, Governor Joseph M. Terrell issued an executive order that the line be resurveyed. The court case was put on hold pending the results.

In August 1907, L. W. Robert, a civil engineer appointed by the governor, presented the state with a newly surveyed plat of the Laurens-Johnson boundary. This recalculated border was found to be to the south of the previously designated line, placing the site of Tyre's murder not in Laurens County but in Johnson. Laurens County objected to the change, bringing suit against Johnson County. On November 7, 1907, Secretary of State Phillip Cook declared the new line the correct one, directing that the survey be recorded as the official county boundary.

The murder indictment issued against Tarbutton and Fluker had been levied by a Laurens County grand jury and was thus invalid. Since it was now officially established that the killing occurred in Johnson County, a series of new hearings and new indictments would be required if the men were to stand trial. With the case in a friendlier jurisdiction, the decision to pursue prosecution was in more familiar hands. Nothing happened. Gus Tarbutton and Joe Fluker remained free men as the details and circumstances of the events were forgotten with the passing years.

The point of origin of the line between the counties was described as being directly opposite the mouth of Big Sandy Creek. On the Johnson County side, the earth rises sharply from the river plain, with the area being known locally as Ring Jaw Bluff. Ironically, some of the same cast of characters would be assembled there nearly two decades later, and Tom

Hardwick would be once again called on to defend two men against a charge of murder at that same Ring Jaw Bluff.[3]

---

[3] For additional information, please see the "Chapter Notes" section near the end of the book.

8

The Rise to the Top

Viewed by the light of the early dawn of the new century, Washington County seemed on the cusp of great things, if it had not already arrived. A May 31, 1903, article in the *Atlanta Constitution* described the county's progress in glowing terms. Written in flowery late-Victorian prose, the seven-column, page-and-a-half piece was full of superlatives and praise for the people, businesses, and history of the place, confidently noting that "if the signs of the times count for anything, her future is roseate with the promise of prosperity far greater even than that of the past." The reporter, clearly skilled at flattery, was Edward Young Clarke, Jr. In later years, his public-relations skills as Imperial Kleagle would propel the newly reborn Ku Klux Klan to national prominence and power. But in these days of bright outlooks, the original Klan of the 1860s was a distant memory, and the turmoil that would fuel its revival was nearly two decades in the future.

Adulation aside, Clarke's words did have basis in reality. As the headline noted, Washington County was indeed the second largest cotton producer in Georgia, and the assertion that "Sandersville, the County Seat, claims many wealthy citizens" was supported by the numerous fine homes and businesses that lined the streets and squares of the county's towns. Despite Sandersville's "accredited" population of only 2,238 citizens, the reporter noted, "it has the appearance of a town possessing at least 5,000 inhabitants."

Sandersville boasted of three banks, two newspapers, between twenty-five and thirty retail stores (plus five wholesale houses), seven "very large manufacturing concerns," two railroads with ten passenger trains each day, not to mention "a poor house, with a large tract of land attached" for those whom prosperity had bypassed. The town's wealthiest citizen at the time was Louis Cohen, a German Jewish immigrant who came to America at age three and moved to Washington County just after the Civil War. In 1903, he owned a bank, was president of the Sandersville Railroad, was a large cotton farmer, and had other diverse business interests. His massive, ornate Victorian home with its turreted porches occupied a prominent position on North Harris Street, a stone's throw from the City Square. He was the man Charlie Rawlings would seek to emulate.

The basis of the wealth of the county was agriculture, and in the words of the local ordinary,[1] "The farmers are healthier and more prosperous than those of any county in the state." In fact, he continued, farmers "are the county's money lenders, offering unlimited sums" to both municipal and private borrowers. Listed prominently among these was C. G. Rawlings, who was described not only as a large planter working "175 plows[2] on his various farms" but also as "a

---

[1] The modern term for "ordinary" is "probate court judge."

[2] The term "plows" was commonly used in Georgia during the first part of the twentieth century to describe the number of acres under cultivation. Although not precisely defined, one plow would equal roughly 30 or 40 acres, indicating that in 1903 Charlie Rawlings was actively farming somewhere between 5,000 and 7,000 acres. This would not have included his entire land holdings at the time, as not all of the acreage of any tract can be used to grow crops, and the figure would not include pastures or timberland. By the latter part of

public spirited citizen [who] always bears his part of any transaction for the public weal." In addition to his farming interests, Clarke also noted Rawlings's livery business was selling more than 2,000 head of horses and mules each year. "Owing to the large size of his trade, the town of Sandersville has reached the point where it sells more stock than any other city of its size in the whole state." Here was clearly a man on the way up.

And Sandersville was not the sole source of pride in the county's thriving economy. Tennille, the railroad junction just three miles to the south, was threatening to surpass the county seat in both size and wealth. With a population of 1,700 but "with all the appearance and enterprise of a city of three or four thousand," it had become so prosperous "that not a dollar of credit business is carried on in the town," a statement that few, if any, other of Georgia's rural villages could match. It had two banks with plans in place for a third, a weekly newspaper, and a yarn mill operating 4,000 spindles. Its streets were lined with imposing homes of landowners and businessmen, several designed and built by the renowned architect Charles Choate. Four railroads funneled goods and commodities from Augusta to the northeast and Dublin, Hawkinsville, and Eastman to the southwest. These lines, which connected to the main Savannah-to-Atlanta route, made Tennille, next to the city of Macon, the busiest depot on the main Central Georgia line.

The way to riches, as Charlie Rawlings knew, was to find a place with a good stream of commerce and figure out a way to take a little cash off the top as it flowed by. With an economy based on agriculture and a hub of operations in the largest and

---

the second decade of the century, Rawlings was said to be operating 600 plows.

C. G. Rawlings

Sandersville and Wrightsville, Ga.

Wholesale and Retail Dealer in

Horses and Mules

Charlie Rawlings began in business as a dealer in horses and mules, soon expanding into other agricultural businesses.

most prosperous town in the area, he found himself in the ideal location. He dominated the market for mules and horses, necessary implements for every farmer. Having branched into the farm supply business, he could effectively eliminate the middleman's cut for his own extensive farming interests. But what of the merchants, large landowners, and other business-men? If money was being made, why not help people manage it—and perhaps make a little profit in the process? In 1905, Charlie Rawlings decided to open the Citizens Bank of Sandersville, the town's fourth such institution.

A discreet news item in the *Sandersville Herald & Georgian* for October 12, 1905, announced that "Mr. C. G. Rawlings, one of our most successful businessmen," had raised $50,000 in subscriptions from potential shareholders and intended to apply to the state for a bank charter. Having lured away J. E. Johnson, the well-respected head cashier, from one of the county's other banks, the newly formed Citizens Bank seemed poised for growth. And grow it did. By late 1908, the bank's assets had reached nearly $195,000, with a surplus fund of $15,000. By mid-1911, assets had reached $272,000 with a surplus of $50,000. In January 1912, the bank declared a 12 percent dividend. Despite offers that more than doubled the amount paid for their original investment, there were no takers among the seventy shareholders, all of whom no doubt believed they could attribute their financial success to Charlie Rawlings.

The bank's success, however, was not due to the entrepreneurial genius of one man. It was more properly attributed to the price of cotton, which hovered just below ten cents a pound for the first half of the new decade, then rose substantially to peak above fourteen cents a pound in 1910. The

Charlie Rawlings's Citizens Bank was located in a building he owned jointly with his brother, Dr. William Rawlings. In this photo from around 1915, the bank is on the lower left, and W. R. Beach's Furniture Company in the middle. To the lower right is the post office. The nurses' residence for the Rawlings Sanitarium was located upstairs.

roller-coaster economy of the 1890s and before seemed to have assumed a steady if gradual upward climb in the new century. Meanwhile, the expansion in wealth was reflected in the growing sophistication of the county's towns. A functional, if static-filled, telephone line connected Tennille and Sandersville. By mid-decade, both towns had municipal water systems and power plants. By the end of the decade, the county had a total of eleven banks and seemed well on its way to Clark's "promise of prosperity far greater even than that of the past."

Charlie Rawlings, now the successful businessman and banker with a vivacious wife and talented children, had settled into a life of comfortable prosperity. There were frequent mentions on the society pages of the *Augusta Chronicle*. Entertaining a prominent newlywed couple in 1898, Rawlings was said to display "genteel manners and [a] jolly nature," while his wife Lula was described as having "a refined but joyful manner." In 1901, he ripped down his windmill and replaced it with the marvel of a new kerosene-fired well pump. In 1904, the local newspaper noted that he had purchased a player piano, with popular tunes magically cranked out by a perforated roll of paper. The following year he served on the building committee of the new Baptist church erected on the corner of Harris and Church streets. At the same time, the local paper noted he had torn down the house on the opposite corner and was building "a handsome two-story dwelling" for his wife and family. He raised purebred trotting horses and registered shorthorn cattle. He entertained lavishly at times, being one of the hosts for more than 2,000 guests invited to his brother's silver wedding anniversary in 1908. By 1909, he was driving a five-passenger Cadillac touring car, the brand that would become his signature in the coming years.

Meanwhile, he was on the cutting edge of the latest advances in farming technology. In 1911, the *Wrightsville Headlight* announced that C. G. Rawlings had ordered a gasoline plow, costing the then-astounding price of $3,000. Capable of tilling up to twenty-four acres a day while consuming some fifty gallons of fuel, it had the potential to increase crop yields by a fourth, not to mention the savings in time and labor. The paper noted, "the new method will be watched with considerable interest by the people of Washington County."

Despite whatever personal or legal foibles may have plagued Charlie Rawlings, he seemed to garner respect from those in high and low places alike. In his autobiography,[3] Berry Gordy, Sr.,[4] recounts the tale of his father's sudden death in 1913. Faced with problems in settling the estate, he turned to "Mr. Charlie Rawlings, the man that ruled the town." His description is telling: "He wasn't the mayor, but he was a

---

[3] Berry Gordy 1979.

[4] Berry "Pop" Gordy, Sr., was the father of Motown Records founder, Berry Gordy, Jr. He was among the many African Americans who joined the Great Migration north in the 1920s, in his case to Detroit, Michigan. His autobiography, with a foreword by Alex Haley, was based on the transcription of a series of tape-recorded sessions collected prior to his death in 1978. I have taken the editorial liberty of correcting the spelling of Charlie Rawlings's name from the original "Charley Rollins" in the book. (One other notable Washington County citizen who became a notable figure on the national scene was Elijah Poole, born in 1897 near Deepstep. He first moved to Macon, where he worked for Cherokee Brick and Tile Company. In 1923, when African-American emigration was at its peak, he moved with his family to Detroit. In the early 1930s, he converted to Islam and eventually changed his name to Elijah Muhammad, rejecting the surname "Poole" as "the name of the white slave-master of my grandfather." He became the supreme leader of the Nation of Islam and a controversial figure in American life and politics.)

millionaire, and whatever he said was always done. He owned the property where the jailhouse and the courthouse was. The town rented from him. He owned most everything, ruled the town, and he was my father's friend." There was a problem with someone having wrongfully placed a lien on a bale of Gordy's cotton. A single phone call from Charlie freed the bale. Gordy had no doubt exaggerated the exact extent of Rawlings's property holdings, but by the early part of the second decade of the century, Charlie did own a sizable portion of the land on and near the City Square, and over the coming years he would acquire more. Power had its privileges.

9

The Seeds of Destruction

For those in small-town Georgia who prospered during the heady years of the second decade of the century, the landscape of the 1930s must have been surreal. The fields, now grown up in broomsage and volunteer pines, the abandoned tenant houses, and the red-clay gullies that funneled water to silt-choked streams had become monuments to a system that seemed to have suddenly failed. But in truth, the forces and factors that would eventually combine to destroy the status quo had been there all the while, unknown to many, misunderstood by others, but ignored by most.

Despite the growth of cities and America's involvement in World War I, much of the nation maintained its agrarian identity until well after the industrial awakening that accompanied World War II. The world of a tenant farmer in rural Georgia in the early part of the century would have encompassed the fields, farms, and villages within a few miles of home. For a small-town merchant or banker, the outlook would have been greater, but for most it was only regional. While newspapers provided some perspective on the world at large, the illiteracy rate was high, and events in New York or London would seem to have little bearing on the timing of rainfall that might make the difference between a bountiful harvest and a winter of slim provisions.

For a historian or economist with the advantages of time and retrospection, the boom that became the grand finale of the cotton economy in Georgia was a mere bubble, and the economic and social set pieces in the endgame clearly pointed down the road to catastrophe. But it is hard to imagine that at the time one could have convinced the average tenant farmer, merchant, or landowner of this inevitability. From their perspective, the system finally seemed to have hit its perfect stride, bestowing the reasonable profits and little luxuries they felt they had been long denied. And for men like Charlie Rawlings, the movers and shakers of small-town Georgia, this period of unparalleled prosperity was tangible validation that their instincts had been correct all along.

If, many years later, you had asked a resident of a dying small town, "What happened?" the likely reply would have been that "the boll weevil" had made cotton farming unprofitable. That in turn led to a cascade of business failures and the stagnation and decline of rural economies. Reality is far more complex. While the invasion of the boll weevil represented a devastating blow, it was only one factor among many that led to the collapse. It is reasonable to speculate that if its arrival in Georgia had occurred some years earlier or later, the outcome would have been quite different.

Georgia's economic system in the early twentieth century was not one that had been designed by businessmen or regulatory fiat; it was one that had evolved, carrying with it the weaknesses and vulnerabilities that would eventually bring it down. These included the system of tenant farming, the dependence on African-American labor, the expansion and subsequent contraction of credit during and following the war years, the lax regulation of the banking system, the phenomenal period of inflation from 1916 through 1920, and the unsustainable bubble in cotton prices that crashed during the Great Recession in 1920. While the eastward march of the boll weevil had reached south Georgia by 1915, the most damaging effects of this pest would not be felt until the 1921, 1922, and 1923 crop years. As such, this plague represented more of a *coup de grace* to an already weakened economy. In fact, for those brave enough to risk planting it, the per-acre yield of cotton had returned to near its pre-weevil levels by the mid- to late 1920s through changes in farming techniques and the aggressive use of insecticides.

One of the early blows was struck on January 5, 1914, when Henry Ford, the owner of the Ford Motor Company, announced a minimum wage of $5.00 per day.[1] The increasing industrialization of the North had resulted in a shortage of skilled workers and rapid turnover in Ford's Michigan plants. Other industries were soon forced to match Ford's offering. As American manufacturing grew in response to World War I, the need for both skilled and unskilled workers grew with it.

While far removed from the cotton fields of Georgia, the news of good jobs and steady pay spread rapidly. By 1920, the majority of Georgia farmers were tenants whose sole equity in their livelihood was whatever remained after the crops were harvested and the year's debts paid. To a farmer eking out a harsh living on fifty cents per day, subject to the vagaries of weather and crop failure, a chance to multiply his income by a factor of ten was a powerful lure. This was especially true for blacks, who faced discrimination and social repression in the rural South. According to the Census of Agriculture for that year, an overwhelming majority of "colored" farmers were tenants. The institutional racism that had so long excluded African Americans from well-paying jobs in northern cities began to fade as the need for workers grew. A slow but steady trickle of men, women, and families began to flow north. In a

---

[1] An inflation-adjusted approximation of this figure in 2011 dollars would be roughly $15 per hour or $120 per day.

few years this would become a torrent known as the Great Migration, depopulating the rural landscape across many counties in the state's Black Belt.

The actions of the federal government under the administration of Woodrow Wilson played a significant role. Although well meaning in their efforts to support agriculture, these actions set the stage for later failure when the economy took a cyclical downturn. Among the accomplishments of the 1913 to 1916 period was the Federal Reserve Act that authorized nationally chartered banks to make loans on farmland. The Federal Reserve's decision to pursue a policy of high marginal rates was later to play a key role in the onset of the Great Recession in 1920. In further assistance of the agricultural segment of the economy, the Federal Farm Loan Act of 1916 was designed to provide stable long-term financing, including the creation of the Federal Land Bank system.

In 1914, a bountiful cotton crop caused a significant drop in prices on various commodity exchanges as bales flooded the market. This led directly to the passage of the United States Warehouse Act of 1916, which effectively monetized receipts for cotton stored in federally certified warehouses. The act's purpose was to permit farmers to store their cotton until the market timing for its sale was optimal, while at the same time allowing them to borrow against its value. The net effect of this was to push banks, even those operating under state charters, into loaning money against cotton. Shortly, banks' balance sheets acquired a new line item in the asset column: "Advances on Cotton." During the years of wildly advancing cotton prices, this figure might have represented twenty to 25 percent of the total assets of some banks in agricultural areas.[2]

---

[2] It is hard not to appreciate the similarity to the line item on banks' balance sheets for mortgage loans in the early 2000s. Indeed,

The expanding economy and the growth in need for credit spurred an explosion in the number of Georgia's banks.[3] From a relatively modest 180 banks in 1900, the total peaked at 798 in 1914. Almost every hamlet seemed to have a bank, often poorly capitalized, lacking deposit insurance, and created in a period of lax regulatory oversight. By the end of the 1920s, more than half of these banks had suspended operations. It is of note that the failure rate, both nationally and in Georgia, was highest in towns with a population of less than 2,500.[4] For many, if not most, the proximate cause would be the coming crash of the agricultural economy.

For those who recall the hyperinflation of the late 1970s during the Carter presidency, and those familiar with the deflation that occurred during the Great Depression of the 1930s, it is often a revelation to discover that the greatest single period of inflation in American history occurred between 1916 and 1920. This was immediately followed by an eighteen-month period of extreme deflation that rivaled that of the entire 1930s. This whipsaw had its origins at least in part in the necessary expansion of credit that preceded and accompanied America's entry into World War I. From the perspective of central bankers in these pre-Keynesian days, inflation was necessarily followed by a period of deflation to restore balance to the currency and economic system.

In 1914 and 1915, inflation was essentially nonexistent, averaging 1 percent each year.[5] In 1916, the Consumer Price Index rose by 10.9 percent, then 18.1 percent, 20.4 percent, and

the situation was analogous, with the primary push for mortgage credit having its origin in federal policies.

[3] Range 1954, 248.

[4] L. J. Alston 1990.

[5] United States Department of Labor n.d.

14.5 percent over the next three years, respectively. (See Appendix, Figure 1.) In the period of recession that followed between January 1920 and July 1921, declining prices and values did not affect all segments of the economy equally. While the Wholesale Price Index fell by 46 percent, consumer prices were estimated to have fallen only about 18 percent.[6] This downturn hit the agricultural sector especially hard. Average net income per farm fell 73 percent during the eighteen months of the recession.[7] There were dramatic declines in commodity prices and the value of farmland, but lesser drops in the cost of production of the now-devalued crops. While farm income increased somewhat during the decade, it fell again with the onset of the Great Depression in 1929. Farm foreclosures increased steadily throughout the 1920s, peaking in 1927.

From the viewpoint of a farmer in rural Georgia, this initial period of inflation was effectively masked by the fact that while prices in general were rising, the value of cotton was rising even faster. But when the downturn arrived in 1920, the increased cost of fertilizer, feed, and fuel had to be weighed against what was now a relatively modest price for cotton, plus the risk that whatever profit might be left would be wiped out by the menace of the boll weevil.

The archaeological record indicates that the insect we know as the Mexican boll weevil was attacking cultivated cotton in Central America more than a thousand years ago.[8] As cotton-based agriculture spread west in the United States, the weevil's range moved north, crossing the Rio Grande near Brownsville, Texas, in 1892. Spreading eastward at a steady

---

[6] Smiley 2010.
[7] Ibid.
[8] P. B. Haney 1996.

rate of less than a hundred miles yearly, it demonstrated its ability to decimate cotton crops, especially in areas with a temperate climate and moderate rainfall. The threat was soon recognized, with the US Department of Agriculture issuing recommendations on weevil control as early as 1901.[9] By 1908, the weevil had spread its destruction across Louisiana, crossing the Mississippi River that year to attack the vast fields of the delta region. By 1911 it had reached Alabama.

Presence of the plague in southwest Georgia was first documented on August 25, 1915, near the village of Boston in Thomas County. By November it had been found in 39 additional counties, covering an area of some 86,000 square miles.[10] Two years later, every cotton-producing county in the state reported evidence of weevil infestation. The insect's deleterious effects on the entire agricultural system were well documented. In 1915, for example, the South Carolina Boll Weevil Commission dispatched a committee to Louisiana and Mississippi to observe firsthand what the state could expect as the insect spread through the rest of the South. They focused their review on areas whose climates approximated those of South Carolina's (and Georgia's) cotton belt. Their report[11] was frightening.

In Louisiana, some 35 percent of cotton gins had closed during the boll weevil years. The figure was similar for Mississippi. Louisiana had lost 44 percent of her cotton oil mills, and Mississippi 36 percent of hers. Perhaps more troubling was the domino effect on rest of the economy. The commission reported the "disastrous effects" on merchants who extended credit to cotton farmers. With cotton planting

[9] United States Department of Agriculture 1901.
[10] P. B. Haney 1996.
[11] The South Carolina Boll Weevil Commission 1921, rev. ed.

decreased and gins and oil mills shuttered, "a large number of the young and able-bodied negroes[12] left the State to seek employment elsewhere." Land values had become "greatly depressed," and banks that had loaned against the land suffered as the value of their collateral plummeted. The report—and numerous other similar warnings—represented the hand writing on the wall. But for farmers in Georgia's cotton country, the price of cotton would more than triple over the next four years, offering a powerful incentive to believe their future would somehow be different.[13]

Georgia's complacency about the boll weevil may have been in part due to the overly optimistic news coming from the US Department of Agriculture. The 1920 Yearbook of Agriculture's section on "Killing Boll Weevils with Poison Dust"[14] asked,

> Can the cotton boll weevil be controlled profitably? If you are a cotton raiser there is hardly anything else you'd rather know. An affirmative answer to the question, eagerly sought since the weevil invaded this country, has been found. The weevil can be controlled by means of a calcium arsenate dust, if the dust is applied at the right season, at the right intervals, and in the right way.

With cotton prices heading for the sky and a solution found, why would anyone choose not to continue planting?

The other factor that no doubt influenced many planters' thinking was the spotty nature of the weevil's damage. While some counties suffered high crop losses, the initial overall

---

[12] See "Sources and Context" section below for an explanation of the author's use of the lowercased term "negro."

[13] Range 1954, 173.

[14] United States Department of Agriculture 1920, 241–52.

effect on the state's production was relatively minor.[15] In 1916, for example, the loss was only 3 percent, and by 1918 only 10 percent. For Georgia, 1919 was the first year in which the boll weevil exacted severe damage on the overall cotton crop, reaching its peak in the 1921–1923 crop years. In Hancock County, for example, a major cotton-producing area and home to the famed Dickson Plantation, between 1915 and 1919, the first five years after the weevil invasion, cotton harvests ranged from 16,078 bales to 22,918 bales per season.[16] To many farmers, the county must have seemed immune to the plague. But in 1920, production dropped to 11,685 bales, falling to 1,509 bales and 710 bales in 1921 and 1922, respectively.

Another important factor was the juxtaposition of the weevil's damage and the onset of the national recession of 1920–1921. Cotton is harvested in the fall, for the most part between September and November. For some counties, 1919 may have been their last good year for cotton production. For others, it may have been among their first bad years. In any case, debts were settled or arrangements made for the coming spring planting season. The growing assurance that the weevil could be controlled with arsenates offered hope for the future. No one realized that instead of improved fortunes, the New Year would herald the beginning of an era of economic decline that would last for decades.

---

[15] Range 1954, 173.
[16] Shivers 1990, 295ff.

10

Farming with Dynamite

The year 1911 ended on a down note for Georgia farmers. Cotton prices, which had been above 14 cents per pound a year earlier, had fallen to 8.9 cents per pound by December, a figure that was significantly less than the average price over the entire first decade of the century. While not a complete disaster, the drop in farm income often meant that loan payments needed to be deferred until the next crop year, with the idea of "getting ahead" put off once again.

Ironically, the downturn was not due to a crop disaster but to an ideal growing season and a remarkably abundant harvest. The *Yearbook of Agriculture* for 1911 reported that the year had produced "the largest cotton crop ever grown." In Georgia, this meant an excess production of more than a million bales over the 1910 crop. Cotton was a commodity, with the price highly subject to the laws of supply and demand. The market had been flooded. Naturally, farmers were wary of the outlook for the coming year.

In January 1912, a large ad appeared in the *Sandersville Georgian*, touting "Farming with Dynamite" and offering a "free demonstration." Two steel-plate etchings ("drawn from actual photographs") showed a field littered with stumps and debris transformed by blasting into a smooth verdant plain of neatly planted crop rows. The copy advised that "the giant force of dynamite" could be used to—among other things—"make old farms produce big crops." Not that big crops were necessarily good; they seemed to have caused the price disaster of the preceding year. Despite this, or perhaps because of simple curiosity, a "large crowd" showed up a couple of weeks later on a farm just south of Tennille to see how this marvelous advance might work.

Using 194 half-sticks of dynamite, 4 boxes of caps, and 400 feet of fuse per acre, engineers from DuPont Powder Company demonstrated in "a plain practical manner" how breaking up land with explosives would "make fine crops, even in spite of two months' drought." The results of "one breaking," at a cost of a mere twelve dollars per acre, would last for seven or eight years. The local witnesses were "deeply impressed," and the engineers went away "quite elated" at their interest. Anything to cut costs while increasing yields was worth trying.

It is unclear whether or not the demonstration made any converts. The front page of the weekly papers, normally the notice board for untimely, bizarre, or violent deaths, reported no one killed or maimed by explosives, a good indication that few farmers found the technique useful. But times were changing rapidly. The cost of "modern" farming with its extensive use of fertilizers was ever increasing, as were other expenses. The Central Fertilizer Company, founded by Charlie Rawlings and other "capitalists" from Washington and surrounding counties, had become a major producer and wholesaler. No matter what the outcome of the crop, the fertilizer that made it grow had to be paid for, and a bit of that would eventually end up in Charlie's pocket.

Most farms were still tilled by mule-drawn plows. Farming was impossible without mules and horses, and for a farmer whose cash income might be a few hundred dollars in a good year, they represented a major investment. Horses generally sold for about 15 to 20 percent less than mules, with the price of the latter heavily influenced by demand and the state of farm economy.[1] In 1890, the average mule sold for about eighty dollars, but this figure had fallen to just above fifty dollars after the disastrous decade of the 'nineties. By 1910, mule prices were back up to about 120 dollars, and by the 1911–1912 years they had reached the previously unheard of price of 160 dollars, more than triple their cost a decade earlier.

For Charlie Rawlings, what he might make in interest charges on loan renewals and increased profits on sales from his livery business would tend to offset any losses he might suffer from farming. The Citizens Bank was doing well and declared a 12 percent dividend in January 1913. Ads proudly offered "absolute safety for your money" and proclaimed "Stock Holders worth $2,000,000." How could anyone not want to do business with a bank owned and operated by those whom success had favored so generously?

As to the sales of mules and horses, Charlie still made several trips a year to the breeding centers of Tennessee and Kentucky, the source of most such livestock used throughout the cotton belt. Many trips took place in the summer and fall, when occasionally he'd drop off his wife Lula in the cool of the north Georgia mountains while he continued further on. Mules, the hybrid progeny of an ass and a mare, were bred for specific uses. In addition to cotton mules, there were sugar mules, draft mules, timber mules, mine mules, and general farm mules, each category having preferred but slight differences in weight, size, and temperament. They were further graded into classes ranging from choice to inferior based on multiple other factors, and then priced accordingly. The animals were shipped in by rail and sold to farmers singly or in

---

[1] Historic information on horse and mule values obtained from the United States Department of Agriculture *Yearbook of Agriculture* series.

quantity. With livery stables in both Sandersville and Wrightsville, Charlie ruled the local market.

The crop years of 1912 and 1913 were better, with cotton near the end of the harvest season selling between twelve and thirteen cents a pound. Not a record, but still an excellent price. The year 1913 would turn out to be especially good. Georgia farmers produced 2.3 million bales of cotton, which they were able to sell at a price that assured a profit. Charlie was in the midst of this market, too. The Dixie Cotton Company, of which he was president and major shareholder, boasted of "offices and agents in every town and county of any size in this part of the state." No matter what the price of cotton was, the company was assured a commission for every bale bought and sold.

The profits from the bank, the cotton factoring business, and the farm supply business, not to mention what he made from the sale of cotton, allowed Charlie to increase his ownership in the Sandersville Railroad. As one of its founders, he had long been a member of the board of directors, but he wanted more. By 1913, majority ownership of the railroad had passed from Louis Cohen to Jeff Irwin, who held the office of president. In September, Charlie Rawlings made a major purchase of the railroad's shares. The board of directors promptly named him vice president. Reporting on the transaction, the *Sandersville Georgian* commented that the railroad was the city's link to the outside world, "and without it, Sandersville would practically be out in the woods." Charlie now controlled a piece of this link.

Encouraged by a resumption of the climb in prices, farmers were looking forward to 1914. In January of that year, Charlie sold an entire railcar load of mules to a Screven County farmer, observing to the local newspaper that "the demand for mules is greater than it has been for several years." The paper reported that he was selling two carloads a week at "prices higher than in former years."

The economy seemed to be improving generally. In February, the Citizens Bank advertised "Plenty of Money to Loan on Real Estate," with both short- and long-term loans available. In March, Charlie's twenty-two-year-old son Fred announced that he had secured the Cadillac, Metz, and Hupmobile agency dealership for Washington, Hancock, Baldwin, and Johnson counties. His father's reputation as a businessman had clinched the deal, but it appeared to be only further validation that the family's seemingly magic touch for making money had been bestowed upon the next generation.

The cotton market continued its positive course. January 1914 prices opened at 11.5 cents a pound, depressed somewhat by the final harvest at the end of the 1913 season. Prices rose steadily, reaching 12 cents per pound by the first of June and 12.2 cents per pound by August. But while across Georgia's cotton belt farmers chopped, hoed, fertilized, and prayed for the late summer thunderstorms that would assure another rich harvest, storm clouds of another sort were gathering half a world away. On June 28, 1914, Archduke Ferdinand of Austria was assassinated in Sarajevo, Bosnia, sparking a series of events that would lead to World War I. The hostilities began in Africa, when on August 7 British and French troops attacked Togoland, at the time a German protectorate. Three days later, German troops attacked British South Africa. On August 1, cotton was selling for 12.2 cents a pound. By September 1, it had plunged to 8.8 cents a pound and continued to fall. By December 1, the end of the harvest season, cotton was selling for 6.7 cents a pound, a figure not seen since the depression of the 1890s.

Cotton was America's leading agricultural export and a major factor in the nation's positive balance of trade. The 1914 crop was shaping up to be a huge one, and would eventually reach 2.7 million bales in Georgia for the year, almost equaling the record crop of 1911. The start of war hostilities led to a plunge in demand, with the massive crop surplus further depressing prices. The credit economy that characterized the South was conducted on a year-to-year basis. Crops were often under lien, leaving farmers little choice but to sell in order to fulfill their debt obligations, as opposed to storing their cotton to wait for the market to improve.

The international crisis caused by the onset of the war had a profound effect on the American economy in general. The Wilson administration responded promptly, setting up a series of conferences to address issues of credit, export, international exchange, transoceanic shipping, etc. On August 18, a conference was called for the next week "to consider the cotton situation." On August 24 a distinguished group of representatives from states heavily involved in "the production, financing, and manufacturing of cotton" met with government officials at the Pan American Building in Washington, DC. In addition to the delegations of the states' experts, the secretary of the treasury, the secretary of agriculture, and the entire Federal Reserve Board (then only a few months old) were in attendance to discuss the emergency. The list from Georgia was a Who's Who of finance, agriculture, and politics. Among the group were C. G. Rawlings and J. E. Johnson of Sandersville, chosen no doubt for their expertise in both farming and finance, if not politics. It is reasonable to speculate that they were nominated by Tom Hardwick, Charlie's attorney and confidant, who at the time had been the congressman from the Tenth District for more than a decade and was the leading candidate for a special election for an open Senate seat from the state.

Johnson, standing just over five feet in height, was a remarkably thin man with a large handlebar moustache and protruding ears. In the decade since Charlie Rawlings had hired him as the cashier and manager of the Citizens Bank, the two men had become friends and fellow investors. Johnson was one of the directors of the Sandersville Railroad and was involved in other farm-related businesses in addition to his full-time job of running the bank. As he was a calm counterpoint to Charlie's aggressiveness, they made a good team. Charlie relied on him heavily.

After meeting for three days, the secretary of the treasury issued a statement directing nationally chartered banks to accept cotton-secured warehouse receipts as collateral for loans, thus allowing farmers some respite from the financial crisis. This decision, later formalized through the United States Warehouse Act of 1916, would prove the undoing of many banks a few years later.

As the crisis deepened into the fall, the Citizens Bank announced its willingness to loan money against cotton at the rate of six cents per pound, or thirty dollars per bale, with the funds guaranteed until July 1915. The loans were to be arranged through the Central Bank and Trust Corporation of Atlanta, the institution founded and owned by Coca-Cola magnate Asa Candler. There were interest and fees, of course, as well as sampling, grading, and storage charges for the cotton. The announcement was signed by C. G. Rawlings and J. E. Johnson, ever adhering to the concept of creating a healthy cash flow and taking a little bit off the top. Even in hard times.

The year 1914 faded with a whimper. As war spread across Europe and cotton prices remained unprofitably low, the Citizens Bank's assets quietly continued to grow. Like a misplaced stick of dynamite designed to loosen and till the soil, what seemed like an excellent idea at the time would later return to haunt bankers across the rural South.

11

Crocodile Tears

Unlike the optimistic mood a year earlier, the dim winter light of January 1915 revealed a dim business outlook. In the first issue of the year, the editor of the *Sandersville Georgian* bemoaned the events of 1914 and the fate of the cotton-based economy:

> Suddenly the impossible happened. The staple which never before had been without a market immediately became unsalable. That which was the most liquid of assets, the equivalent almost of gold, became a weight on the hands of its owners. Incidentally millions of persons who had given months of toil and spent millions of dollars in the planting and cultivating of what promised to be the richest crop in the history of the south were confronted with ruin.
>
> To realize the magnitude of this commercial tragedy it is necessary to understand not only that practically every branch of endeavor in the south is affected by cotton, but that instantly the cotton manufacturing industry of the world was demoralized, scores of cotton traders were brought to the verge of bankruptcy and banks and merchants, whose business was as sound as human effort can make it, had to face losses of staggering proportions.

The Citizens Bank had gambled and—depending on the future price of cotton—stood to gain or lose dramatically. Overall, assets were up by about 25 percent compared to a year earlier, but, more important, the value of outstanding loans

had more than doubled, much of which was accounted for by
"Advances on Cotton." As might be expected, many farmers
held on to their bales, refusing to sell for a market price below
their cost of production. As a consequence, the bank's deposits
had decreased significantly. At the end of 1914, the Citizens
Bank had outstanding loans amounting to nearly three times
the total deposits. Much of the money had been borrowed from
other banks. The roulette wheel had been spun.

A prominent but somber notice from the bank appeared in
the same issue of the *Georgian*. Signed by C. G. Rawlings and
the entire board of directors, it stated, "On account of the
depressed condition of the country, and because many of the
customers are holding Cotton, the Directors voted to postpone
the paying of dividends until a later date." In perspective, it
was a somewhat strange advertisement. The economic future
of many—if not most—of the bank's borrowers depended on
the willingness of this group of wealthy men to continue to
extend credit. While privately they might have felt otherwise,
the directors realized it would be unseemly to appear to be
profiting from the economic misfortunes of others. Citing their
motto of "Safety and Strength," they realized they could wait a
few months for their money.

Despite whatever misgivings the South might have about
the economy, preparations for the spring planting season
began once again. The predictions were that farmers would cut
back somewhat on their cotton acreage. Fertilizer prices began
to inch up as a result of the war-related competition for raw
materials. Otherwise, it was back to business as usual. There
was news of a possible new railroad line to connect Atlanta
and Savannah. In March, the stockholders of the Sandersville
Railroad again elected Jeff Irwin as president and C. G.
Rawlings as vice president. With Charlie's blessing no doubt,

his first cousin, twenty-nine-year-old Benjamin J. ("Ben") Tarbutton, was appointed general manager. Charlie's son Fred continued to do well also. In addition to being the leading automobile dealer of the area, he now held the Gulf Gasoline franchise, serving the growing demand by importing fuel in tank carloads.

Even though America was more than two years away from her formal entry into the European conflict, war news dominated the local headlines. The carnage was a distant reality for most. The sinking of the Cunard ocean liner *RMS Lusitania* in May with the loss of nearly 1,200 lives elicited an ad from Jackson's 5&10¢ Store proclaiming "Lusitania Sunk. Also The Prices at Jackson's." By the first of May, cotton was again selling for well above eight cents a pound. The Citizens Bank resumed its usual ads boasting of "the largest capital and surplus of any bank in Washington County" and that its "stockholders are worth over $1,500,000.00." As the early cotton crop began to come in, prices rose, breaking the eleven cents per pound mark by October and remaining there through the end of the year. The doomsayers of a few months earlier had been silenced and, for the moment, forgotten.

Even the late summer announcement of the long-anticipated arrival of the boll weevil in Georgia failed to dim enthusiasm. The Dixie Cotton Company bought a thousand bales from a businessman-farmer in Bartow for the comfortable price of 11.5 cents a pound. In that thriving small railroad stop some twenty-odd miles southeast of Sandersville, the merchants wanted "the world to know good times are now on," inviting the public to explore the "bargains galore."

Whatever the locals might have thought, the rising economic outlook was in large part due to the war. The resulting loosening of credit allowed many farmers to avoid the fate of bankruptcy that might otherwise have resulted from the crisis of the preceding year. But the growing demands for war material were also planting the seeds of inflation. The British government was buying thousands of mules on the open market in Atlanta, all to be shipped to the western front. In September, the German government cabled Georgia senator Hoke Smith, offering sixteen cents a pound for a million bales of cotton delivered to Bremen. They had already made a cash deposit with the American consulate in Berlin. With the onset of hostilities in Europe, cotton's value had risen as an essential component in the production of the explosive nitrocellulose for use in military munitions. In order to avoid violating American neutrality, the purchasing firms were willing to "guarantee" (with a wink and a nod) that the cotton would not be put to military use.

The railroads, the lifelines of commerce and trade, reported near the year's end that "general business is much better." Both the Central of Georgia and the Augusta Southern railways issued somewhat incidental reports on the wide variety of clays found along their rail beds. Largely unexploited, there were massive deposits of pure, white, high-grade kaolin and fire clays, plus the related ore known as bauxite, the primary source of aluminum. It was speculated that in the future, these mineral deposits would serve as the basis of a large mining industry. For the moment, however, there was no need to dig into the earth any depth greater than that needed to grow cotton, the world's white gold.

By the year's end, all was well. Charlie Rawlings advertised "Christmas Mules," having just received a carload of fine animals from Tennessee. Predicting a good year to follow, he observed, "Mules are high and will probably go higher as the season advances." The Citizens Bank placed a large ad announcing the tenth anniversary of the founding of the bank, affirming that "today it is stronger and in better condition than at any time during its existence." The gamble had paid off, and the funds borrowed from other banks were repaid. At year's end the bank declared a 24 percent dividend.

A few weeks later, a notice appeared in the *Georgian* advertising for sale "one Cadillac Touring Car, good as new, driven about 10,000 miles, equipped with electric lights and starter, [and] new tires all around." While Sandersville was a wealthy town, there were few men who could afford such a fine (and expensive) vehicle, and even fewer who might choose to trade it in such good condition. Charlie Rawlings had done well for himself, and, as the largest stockholder of the Citizens Bank, the 24 percent dividend allowed him such luxuries. The rich were becoming richer.

12

"Colored People Are Buying Automobiles"

The real cotton boom began in 1916. For the rural South, it was in many ways a strange time. The papers were full of news of the European war, but to most it was a distant storm whose sole effect thus far seemed to be a constant gentle breeze that lifted the local economy. Demand for cotton remained strong as prices rose steadily during the course of the year. The price of 11.4 cents per pound in January climbed incrementally to 14.6 cents by the first of September.

While Charlie Rawlings was enjoying his wealth, his son Fred was working on his own financial empire. With his local car dealerships and oil franchise profitable and growing, Fred had taken on a business partner, Ben Holt. Ben was the son of Lake B. Holt, president and owner of the local First National Bank and another of Sandersville's wealthier men. Holt lived in an imposing Choate-designed house[1] on North Harris Street, in the midst of the other bankers and businessmen who had "done well." By 1916, he was in his late fifties and, like Charlie, was intent on making certain his heirs shared in his entrepreneurial success.

---

[1] Appropriately named "Sunny-side."

"Sunny-side" Residence of Mr. L. B. Holt, Sandersville, Ga.

Lake B. Holt was Charlie Rawlings's competitor and president of the county's other leading bank. He would later become the receiver for Charlie's estate. His Choate-designed home on North Harris Street was indicative of his wealth.

In early March, it was announced that the Rawlings and Holt boys had just returned from Detroit, where they had secured the Cadillac franchise for the entire state, and that they planned to open a showroom in Atlanta. Their new dealership on Peachtree Street—just three blocks from the state capitol—was wildly successful. By the fall they were selling some fifteen new cars a week with orders booked months in advance. The *Georgian* reported that they had "sold more Cadillacs than any other firm south of the Mason and Dixon line."

Automobiles, which had been far beyond the reach of most a decade earlier, were now beginning to become common, and used cars were entering the market as buyers traded up. The trickle-down effect seemed to have reached even the lowest rung of society, as the *Georgian* reported near the start of the harvest season with the front-page headline, "Colored People Are Buying Automobiles." Noting that the "high price of cotton gives them opportunities for luxuries," the writer commented approvingly that, "They are enjoying the general prosperity that prevails and are entitled to the fruits of their labors."

The community at large was thriving. Sandersville now had a population of 3,140. A spring "Booster Edition" of the paper boasted of fourteen dry goods and grocery stores, four drug stores, three furniture stores, and others—a dramatic increase from a decade earlier. Municipal water and sewerage was now available to those in town. The unpaved streets were said to be lined with "beautiful shade trees and flowers" and "splendid paved sidewalks," though the article neglected to mention that they turned into a muddy mire when it rained. A "building boom" was reported in the city, created both by houses for the newly wealthy and by expanded commercial construction. Befitting his place in society, the article singled out C. G. Rawlings as a "Capitalist, and one of Washington County's wealthiest citizens and one of the largest landowners and planters in the state." In those days, it was an honor to be called a "capitalist."

The positive outlook led to the formation of a Chamber of Commerce, which elected J. E. Johnson, the Citizens Bank's cashier and Charlie Rawlings's right-hand man, as its first president. Entertaining the chamber members a few months later in his "handsome home" on West Church Street (also designed by Charles Choate), Johnson addressed the growth of Sandersville and Washington County and the acclaim and positive publicity the area was receiving from around the state. The future seemed endlessly bright.

For whatever positive outlook the business community might have, there were signs of changing times and trouble ahead. Despite the fact that the United States had shipped nearly a million mules and horses to Europe since the beginning of the war, the animals' domestic price had begun to drop as farmers shifted to automobiles and gasoline-powered tractors. Speaking on cotton and the economy, W. P. G. Harding, a member of the Federal Reserve Board, warned of the risk of inflation. On a local level this was manifest by the *Georgian* increasing its subscription price from $1.00 per year to $1.50 in April, and again to $2.00 per year in December. The boll weevil was reported to be "actively at work in the county." A local man traveling through the "weevil section" in south Georgia found "acres of cotton just completely ruined" and that "the negroes are leaving in droves." All of these should have been signs of trouble to come, but in Washington County, farmers continued to rely on cotton as the primary crop, either ignoring or failing to understand what the future would hold.

They had good reasons to suspend disbelief, at least for the near future. The US Department of Agriculture reported that it had discovered a way of "destroying the boll weevil," and hoped that within a year the pest could be controlled. Further testing was said to be needed. European demand for American cotton continued to grow, fueled not only by the needs of war but also by the sinking of cotton-laden merchant ships by the German U-boat fleet. As an added economic bonus, the war years had brought with them a growing demand for cottonseed. Once regarded as no more than trash and often used as fill for rain-washed gullies, the value of the oil and protein in the seed had led to a doubling in price by the end of the 1915–1916 cotton season. When the stunning value of cotton lint was added to the newfound income from its seeds, there seemed to be little reason to seriously consider diversifying to other crops.

Most important, however, was the simple fact that the prices paid for cotton continued to increase. By November 1916, lint was selling for 18 cents a pound and, by the first of December, 19.6 cents. Profits were made and debts were paid. The Citizens Bank's deposits by year's end had soared to 80 percent higher than a year earlier. Ads announced that the bank "is loaded with money," and had invested in a new mechanical adding and subtracting machine.

While those in town did well, those in the country also thrived. In nearby Johnson County, Gus Tarbutton had settled into the comfortable role of gentleman-planter. The killings of 1906 seemingly now forgotten, he lived with his wife and son in a large, comfortable two-story white frame house with a shaded, wrap-around porch set in a grove of mature oak trees and surrounded by a clean-swept yard. Fronting on the main Sandersville to Dublin road, it was near the intersection of the muddy track connecting Wrightsville to the Oconee River, giving the area the name of Tarbutton's Crossroads. Farming had been good to Gus. In 1910 he owned 2,250 acres, according to local tax records. By 1914 he owned nearly 4,000 acres, and by 1918 between 7,000 and 8,000. His property fronted on the river, and the area known as Ring Jaw Bluff began to be referred to by some locals as "Tarbutton's Bluff."

The Tarbutton farmstead was the center of a busy cotton plantation. He ran a country store to furnish[2] his tenants and customers, and farmed enough cotton to have his own gin, which cleaned not only his crop but also that of other farmers in the area. There was a harness and blacksmith shop, mule barns, and other barns for storage of feed, fertilizer, and horses. Further afield, his property was dotted with tenant houses interspersed in a maze of dirt tracts between vast fields of cotton.

Locally, rumors had it that Gus made so much money that he would steal off and bury it in the woods because he did not trust banks. In truth, he banked with his cousin, Charlie Rawlings. Just before Christmas 1916, a man named John C. Todd presented a check to the Citizens Bank of Sandersville bearing the forged signature of Gus Tarbutton. Obviously not realizing that Charlie was Gus's cousin, he was arrested to be held without bail pending the next term of court the following spring. Todd's pleas to Gus that he had a wife and child and

---

[2] The word "furnish" used in this context refers to a merchant or landlord supplying not only farming needs but also basic supplies to tenants and/or sharecroppers, usually under a credit agreement under which the debt would be repaid either in cash or in crops. Small-town merchant Will Varner, one of Faulkner's characters in *The Hamlet*, represents a classic, if overblown, literary example of a furnisher.

would offer to pay him "any sum that he would name" to drop the charges fell on deaf ears. An attempted crime had been committed, and the offender should pay. Unless, of course, he had a rich cousin who could buy his way out of jail, as had been Gus's good fortune in the Lecher Tyre killing a decade earlier.

13

The Spoils of War

A s 1916 progressed and drew to a close, America's uncertain attitude toward the European war shifted toward realization that involvement in the conflict was inevitable, and preparations must be made. The industrialized North was already directly benefiting from increased production and exports necessitated by the war, as had the South from a steady and rising market for its prime export of cotton. Germany's relentless U-boat war against shipping bound for Britain, stories of atrocities committed by occupying armies, and the horrific loss of life on the stalemated Western Front served to convince many Americans that the time had come for Uncle Sam to step in on the side of the Allies.

In the South, the sentiment favored intervention. Cotton prices stayed high, driven in large part by the demands of the war. A study by the Central of Georgia Railway found that the average farmer in the cotton belt had made a profit of more than $21 per acre in 1916, a figure that was likely to equal or exceed the amount he had originally paid for the land. The British government was now buying cotton directly, placing an order in February 1917 for 20,000 bales to be shipped from the port of Savannah. The outlook was good.

The impending war, however, had opened rifts between the North and the South. The South's ability to produce cotton and other farm commodities was highly dependent on the availability of labor, both hired workers and tenant farmers. As the need for industrial workers in the North grew, accompanied by a dramatic decline in European immigration, the South seemed a fertile hunting ground for new labor, especially among the black population. The ingrained racism that had discouraged African-American migration to the North was now being supplanted by the simple economic need for manpower.

A January 1917 front-page article in the *Georgian* announced, "Labor Agents at Work in This Section of the State."[1] A recruiter employed by "northern manufacturers" had been discovered working in the Sandersville area "for the purpose of inducing the colored population to go north." He was said to have made "glowing promises," and found a number of potential emigrants. In case the carrot of good wages was not enough, the blacks were also told "that if they decline the offer the white people of the south intend to kill them if they should remain here until May 1st." But, as the writer warned, "If our colored citizens would read the daily papers and see where their race is rapidly returning from the northern states, they would not be so anxious to go."

By way of graphic example, the *Georgian* quoted a recent story in the *Macon Telegraph* recounting the fate of a group of "colored people" from Rochelle, Georgia: "Of the party consisting of twenty-five negroes who left this section a few weeks ago for Pennsylvania, seven have returned and report that the other members died from the severe cold and that when any of their race died, the hearts were taken from the bodies and the corpses burned." Over the following weeks, the paper continued to report similar horror stories of local blacks who had made the mistake of "going north" but somehow managed to survive and make it home. Jim Kelsey, described

---

[1] This was juxtaposed next to a prohibition piece titled "Rattlesnake Is Less Dangerous Than Liquor."

as a colored farm hand who left for Pennsylvania, returned two months later to report that indeed he got "bigger wages, but had to pay still bigger for anything that he bought." And worse, perhaps, was the revelation that "everything had to be paid spot cash." He said that among the "eight hundred negroes in the hospitals in Philadelphia, many have died, and others cannot get in because they are overcrowded."

Charley Williams, a "young colored man" who had gone to Pennsylvania to work in various factories, acknowledged receiving from $2.50 to $4.00 per day for his labor but having to subsist on "light bread and pickled beef, which he described as abominable." He reported that "many of the negroes suffered from pneumonia and a large number had died from exposure to the severe cold, while others had to have their arms, legs and ears amputated on account of freezing." Williams said he had no intentions of returning north, the implication being that others should heed his example. The situation was so threatening that the Georgia Commissioner of Agriculture traveled to Washington, DC, to discuss what the federal government might do to help stop the "negro exodus." He was told that such was "a state problem" and the legislature needed to pass "drastic laws against illegitimate operations of labor agents."

Though many blacks found good jobs, not all areas of the North were so hospitable. In late May, the Cincinnati, Ohio, police deported a party of "five hundred negroes from Central Georgia," who were in "a near starving condition" after having been induced to travel to Michigan and discovering "that the labor agents [had] swindled them with rosy stories of big wages which never existed for white or black." The "desperate half-starved newcomers" were accused of causing "a smallpox epidemic and other diseases," resulting in "the city and state and federal authorities…unitedly bitterly opposing the negro influx." Despite all, the exodus continued.

With the declaration of war against Germany and her allies in early April, the mood turned to one of intense patriotism. The call for universal registration of men potentially eligible for military service did not discriminate between black and white. There were fears, both spoken and unspoken, that training and arming southern negroes could potentially destabilize the status quo. One of the proximate reasons for America's entry into the war was the infamous Zimmerman Telegram, intercepted, decrypted, and revealed to the world by British intelligence. Arthur Zimmerman, the German foreign minister, sought an alliance with Mexico if the United States entered the war on the side of Britain. In the telegram, he proposed the return of former Mexican territories in the southwest should Germany be victorious over the Allies. In addition to this, there were rumors that Germany was making "efforts to induce the negroes of the south to revolt against the United States government."

Within days of the official declaration of war, the *Georgian* carried a frontpage article under the headline, "Ringing Note from a Negro Uplifter." The piece reported the words of Robert E. Clay, described as "a negro orator and uplift worker among men and women of his race and recognized as a champion of the Booker Washington idea." Clay said he could not "conceive of the disloyalty of the Negro race," promising to "fight and die, if need be for American honor and the protection of American homes, white and black."

The attitude had now changed from simply preventing the blacks from leaving the South to one in which both their loyalty and their willingness to continue farm labor were assured. Meetings were held around the state that stressed "the importance of raising food supplies." The Washington County courthouse hosted such a convocation of "colored citizens meet[ing] as patriots" in early June, just prior to the date on which all men of military age were required to register for possible conscription. The county school superintendent and a local judge—both white—"delivered addresses in which they gave some splendid advice to the colored people," followed by a pledge of allegiance to the American flag and a resolution of support for the war effort.

If patriotism were to fail, however, other methods of assuring loyalty were available. Later in the summer, "it became known" that one Zeb Gilmore, a negro, "had openly boasted of what he intended to do after all the white men had gone to the European war. His boasts naturally aroused a great deal of indignation and a crowd was soon gathered to inflict punishment." He was arrested—allegedly on a charge of beating his wife—and while being escorted to jail was seized by the crowd. The next morning his bullet-riddled body was found tied to a tree. A coroner's jury quickly rendered a verdict that his death had been "caused by parties unknown."

The paranoia was not directed against blacks alone. In late March, a few days before President Wilson's address to Congress requesting a declaration of war, two young German men were spotted in Sandersville, "pretending to be travelers seeing the sights of the world." A local farmer, loading some hogs and cattle at a railway siding, questioned them and thought they were acting "peculiar." A few days later he recognized a photo of the same two men, arrested in Atlanta "on the blanket charge of suspicion." The authorities revealed that on searching their room, they found "a lot of papers in German writing," the mere possession of which seemed sufficient to believe they were up to no good. There was a rumor of a possible plan to destroy a warehouse in Atlanta holding cotton bound for Britain, and another of a plot to blow up a dam that supplied the city's water.

A couple of weeks later—after the formal declaration of war—the local paper warned the citizens of Washington County to "look out for spies at every turn of [the] road." German agents were said to be traveling throughout the country "for the purpose of doing all the devilment of which the German mind is capable." The article continued, "They will not hesitate to poison wells and water works systems, scatter typhoid germs wherever they go, or destroy public utilities of every description." Riding on the tide of patriotic nationalism, D. W. Griffith's *The Birth of a Nation*, in part depicting the destruction of the South by Sherman's hoards, played to large crowds at the local school auditorium.[2] Germany would not be allowed to do the same.

War and spies aside, Charlie Rawlings was making money. Deposits in the Citizens Bank would more than double during the course of the year as the price of cotton reached nearly twenty-five cents a pound by July and nearly twenty-nine cents by the end of December. The boll weevil, while present in the county, seemed to have had little practical effect on the cotton crop. The bank began to advertise "Long Term Loans" of three to five years on real estate, a sure sign that the boom was due to last at least that long. Money was also available for home building, again a long-term investment for not only the borrower but also the bank. The livery business was also doing well. Army mule buyers passed through town looking for more stock to support the campaign on the Western Front.

---

[2] *The Birth of a Nation* (silent film), dir. D. W. Griffith, 1915, based on *The Clansman* (novel and play by Thomas Dixon, Jr.).

With the surge in the economy came inflation.[3] It had been almost nonexistent in 1914 and 1915, but by mid-1916 prices had begun to rise sharply, reaching an annualized monthly rate of approximately 12 percent by the end of the year. By spring 1917, the annualized rate had reached nearly 19 percent and remained at or above this level though the remainder of the year. While the papers had noted early in 1917 that prices were "four to five times higher than a year ago on many products," this was attributed to "the enormous demands of Europe," and seemed to be considered a temporary phenomenon. There were other factors that likely hid the problem from the average small-town farmer or merchant. First, the increase in the price paid for cotton was far greater than the overall rise in prices, resulting in a general increase of wealth in both real and inflation-adjusted dollars. (See Appendix, Figures 2, 3, and 4.) Second, while the "near cashless" society of the late nineteenth century had in various ways passed, many of life's basic needs were still homegrown or home acquired. Most homes had large gardens, and most families bought local meat and produce. These prices were more likely to remain nearly stable.

As farmers began the cotton harvest season in the fall, a news piece in the *Sandersville Progress* reminded readers of the

---

[3] Broadly defined, inflation refers to the decline in the value of a currency when compared to the market value/price of certain goods or services. When the currency loses value, this is referred to "inflation" (or "deflation" if the currency gains value under similar circumstances). As such, blanket statements about the rate of inflation are nearly impossible to make accurately, as different goods and services may increase (or decrease) in value/price somewhat independently. The figures given for "inflation" and/or "deflation" in this work are based on the Consumer Price Index, first measured in 1914 under the Federal Reserve Act.

valuable clay deposits that lay beneath their feet. People "are walking over hidden wealth almost every day," the article said, and extolled landowners to have their property examined for minerals, especially bauxite, which was described as "very valuable." Most ignored the news; cotton farming was far more profitable.

Near year's end, the wildly successful "former Sandersville boys," Ben Holt and Fred Rawlings, visited town in a new 1918 Cadillac that drew a large crowd on the City Square. They were on a statewide tour of their various dealerships, and reported that demand for cars was so intense that newly wealthy buyers, unwilling to wait for routine delivery, wanted them shipped from Detroit by express train. Their fathers' touch for making money had clearly been passed to the next generation. But that was not to say that the fathers themselves were any less interested in expanding their own wealth. In early December, Charlie Rawlings sold 1,000 bales of cotton for the then-astounding price of twenty-eight cents a pound, an accomplishment of sufficient merit to warrant a front-page headline in the local paper. He revealed to the reporter that he had more than 2,000 additional bales of the season's crop yet to be sold.

Two weeks later the headlines read, "Change in Ownership [of the] Sandersville Railroad." Jeff Irwin, the railroad's president, had sold his stock to Charlie Rawlings and J. E. Johnson. The directors promptly bestowed on Charlie the office of railroad president and on Johnson that of vice president. Charlie's first cousin, Ben Tarbutton, continued in the position of general manager. With family and trusted employees in charge, Charlie could be certain the business was well managed.

At year's end, a scant decade and a half after the *Atlanta Constitution* had referred to him merely as a "public spirited citizen," Charlie Rawlings had definitively surpassed Louis Cohen as the area's richest man. He owned and farmed tens of thousands of acres of cotton, a source of immense wealth. His bank was thriving, with deposits at an all-time high. He owned controlling interest in the local railroad. His only living son, in business now on his own, was successful. There were few clouds on the horizon. What could possibly go wrong?

14

The Hand of Providence

While the frozen trench war continued on Europe's Western Front through the winter of 1917–1918, things seemed positively rosy on the home front in Georgia. Sandersville's two largest financial institutions, Charlie Rawlings's Citizens Bank and Lake Holt's First National Bank, both declared 12 percent dividends, the generous amount attributed to "remarkably fine management." And were the ability to produce such fine businessmen not enough, Miss Frances Jordan—formerly of Sandersville but now living in New York City—was selected as "the prettiest girl in America," an honor that earned her photograph a spot on a calendar to be widely distributed among troops serving in the military.

If the local papers were to be believed, even the negroes were happy, or at least participating in "frolics," one of which resulted in the shooting of a man named Whistler on Gus Tarbutton's farm in Johnson County. They seemed to be supporting the war effort; Albert Williams, a farmer from the Davisboro community, was "the first Colored Citizen in the State to become a member of the One Thousand Dollar Club," having purchased that much in war savings stamps.

The financial support of Georgia's African-American population may have been welcomed, but it did little to change their perceived place in society. The Selective Service Act of

The Choate-designed First National Bank Building, owned by its president, Lake B. Holt, was the most prominent building on Sandersville's City Square.

1917 allowed universal conscription and required all men of military age—irrespective of race—to register for the draft. Tom Hardwick, now one of Georgia's senators, reflected the mood of many in Georgia with his opposition to the entire process. In addition to the potential loss of farm labor, he feared endangerment of "the supremacy of the Caucasian control in the South, for it is unreasonable to expect that ten million negroes can be trained to arms without utterly destroying that submissive and contented spirit with which their race takes and accepts the subordinate position it must occupy unless the South is to be hybridized and mongrelized."[1]

For whatever empowerment military service might offer, it was made abundantly clear to local blacks that nothing had changed. "There seems to be an impression among the colored people that a soldier at home on furlough may commit any crime he sees fit and no punishment will be meted out to him," the *Sandersville Progress* opined. But, the writer continued, "Sheriffs...are ready to answer calls from any part of the county to arrest any person of any color, either soldier or civilian that commits a crime in this county." Order, the old order, must be maintained. The lynching of Zeb Gilmore—taken by the mob from the sheriff's custody—was still fresh in everyone's mind.

For those who were part of the system, however, the bounty continued. The Sandersville Railroad made two large purchases of land near the City Square with plans to build additional warehouses, a coal yard, an icehouse, and other improvements. With this acquisition, Charlie Rawlings now controlled even more of the town. His family was prospering as well. His brother William's hospital, known as the Rawlings Sanitarium, had achieved a reputation extending "throughout

---

[1] Hardwick, 1917.

the Southern states." The current patient capacity had been overwhelmed, and additional land was being acquired for a facility to treat "colored patients."

Despite the increasing use of gasoline-powered equipment, the mule remained the mainstay of farm power. Wartime demand for mules had so cut into the supply that prices were once again on the rise. It was predicted that within two years good mules would be selling for $600 each, and farmers were encouraged to purchase now while they were still affordable.

Community support for the war effort remained strong. The papers were full of ads for liberty bonds. *The Kaiser—The Beast of Berlin* played at the local school auditorium,[2] with newspaper ads proclaiming that "America and Civilization must rid the world of this overbearing, autocratic, fiendish murderer of humanity." Even those whom success had favored joined the war effort. Fred Rawlings temporarily put his automobile business aside to be commissioned as a lieutenant, arriving in France in September 1918 as a member of the American Expeditionary Forces.

With demand good, cotton prices remained more or less stable for 1918, at times pushing thirty-two cents a pound but averaging around twenty-eight cents for the year. There were no reports of the boll weevil in the county until near the end of September, too late to do any significant damage to the crop. In this, the fourth year after the arrival of the feared intruder in Georgia, Washington County seemed somehow charmed, thus far immune to the long-feared ravages of the pest. By mid-October, cotton warehouses were overflowing, and ads were placed telling farmers there was no more space for the bounteous crop.

---

[2] *The Kaiser—The Beast of Berlin* (silent film), dir. Rupert Julian, 1918.

With the Armistice in November, traders predicted a new surge in European demand and speculated that by mid-1919 cotton would be bringing forty-five cents a pound. But, while 1918 cotton prices hovered in a narrow range, inflation remained relentless. The Consumer Price Index closed the year more than 20 percent higher than twelve months earlier. Those who reveled in cotton's climb seemed to ignore inflation's erosive effect on its true worth. Cotton was deemed to be the equivalent of hard currency. The Citizens Bank ended the year with nearly a quarter of its total assets listed as "Advances on Cotton."

As farmers prepared for the 1919 crop year, the outlook was bullish but tempered. The demand for mules was "exceeding all expectations," but a brief lull and drop in the price of cotton had given pause to some. Costs had risen to the point that it was now estimated that it cost a farmer about twenty cents to produce a pound of cotton. When the price dropped to twenty-four cents by the first of March, there was talk of holding the crop until it returned to a higher value. By May, however, cotton bounced back, breaking the thirty-cent barrier by June. With the price now predicted to go far higher by the end of the year, local farmers intensified their operations in anticipation of windfall profits. At Dr. William Rawlings's 15,000-acre Ferncrest Plantation just north of town, fields were even being tilled at night with illumination from the headlights of gasoline-powered tractors.[3] A new ginnery capable of

---

[3] Dr. Rawlings was an innovator in other areas of farming also. He constructed what was said to be the world's largest circular barn, built around a central silo and designed for efficiency in feeding his large dairy herd. The barn, which burned in the 1950s, was for years a notable landmark for travelers passing through Sandersville.

FERN CREST DAIRY, NEAR SANDERSV.LLE, GA.

Ferncrest Dairy, part of a 15,000-acre spread owned by Charlie Rawlings's brother, Dr. William Rawlings, was known for its huge circular barn designed to efficiently feed cattle. It was said to be the world's largest of its type.

producing 125 bales of cotton a day was scheduled to be completed prior to the harvest season.

This year, the boll weevil appeared early in Washington County, with reports of wide infestation by early summer. Farmers responded—when they could afford to—by multiple applications of lead or calcium arsenate, compounds that had been found to control the weevil when properly applied. The cost, however, which was estimated by the State College of Agriculture to be more than $16 per acre, cut deeply into final profits, as did inflation, which averaged more than 15 percent for the full year. With cotton closing out the harvest season near thirty-seven cents a pound, none of this seemed to matter.

With the general increase in prosperity, many were uncertain as to what to do with their newfound wealth. Others, perhaps those not directly involved in the gold mine of agriculture, may have felt somehow bypassed by the good fortune fate had bestowed on their friends and colleagues.[4] In May 1919, an unbelievable opportunity presented itself to those seeking a quick shortcut to riches. Oil had been discovered in Washington County. The story, as recounted in a large-type, half-page ad in the May 9 issue of the *Progress*, was as follows: In January, a gang of prison convicts digging a new road through the plantation of W. R. Beach (coincidentally, the same man who'd spotted the German spies in Sandersville nearly two years earlier) had discovered what appeared to be a patch of petroleum seeping from the ground. After some months of investigation and due diligence, the Middle Georgia Oil & Gas Company had been founded, with offices in the prestigious Flatiron Building in Atlanta.

---

[4] Not unlike those who, by 1999, had failed to invest in tech stocks, or those who in 2006 had foolishly avoided the real estate market.

The evidence seemed incontrovertible. A consultant chemist and a professor at Mercer University had been sent samples of the seepage. Both agreed that the specimens submitted to them were consistent with hydrocarbons and "probably [came] from some gas and oil deposit." Within weeks, a parade of alleged oilmen from Texas, Oklahoma, and Louisiana, like the Magi of old, had arrived to see for themselves this marvelous discovery. Each pronounced the seepage a sure sign of an underlying pool of oil, sure to bring obscene riches to those fortunate enough to "get in on the ground floor."

The citizens of Washington County—prior to any others— were being offered the opportunity to invest in this new enterprise. To allay any concerns potential investors might have, the directors were all local men, the most prominent of whom was Lake Holt, president of the First National Bank, as well as an attorney, the owner of the local Coca-Cola Bottling Company, and three planters including Mr. Beach, on whose farm the discovery had been made. All were described as "conservative successful businessmen of the highest integrity." Beach served as president, and as the months went by he became the spokesman and public face of the company.

The fact that W. R. Beach was involved in the oil exploration business should not have surprised anyone who knew him. A profile in the local paper some two years earlier described him as a native of Washington County, where he raised cotton and watermelons for years before expanding his business interests to town shortly after the turn of the century. He was the local Buick dealer and operator of the Beach Garage ("with modern equipment and skilled mechanics"), all done while running a combination furniture store and undertaking establishment on the side with a "superior stock" of coffins, caskets, and burial robes.[5] On his farm, he bred Hampshire hogs. This was also the location of the Beach Mill, producing the "best" meal for cooking when not grinding feed for farmers.

The half- and full-page ads, cleverly written and full of screaming headlines and anecdotal examples of fortunes made by ordinary folks in the oil business, continued weekly. For thirty-five dollars, an investor could purchase a lot "large enough for sinking an oil well." The purchaser would not only have the right to drill his or her own well but would also share equally in any profits made by the company on oil that was recovered from company wells, as yet to be drilled. Within three weeks, more than 300 lots had been sold locally, and in less than a month, more than 600. A partial listing of the names and occupations of the buyers spanned the rungs of Washington County's social ladder. Ranging from physicians, attorneys, and bankers to painters, cab drivers, and salesmen, all seemed destined to follow in the footsteps of a man named Johnson, who had bought a small tract of oil land for only $190 and later refused an offer of $200,000 as inadequate. Or perhaps those of the Olsan brothers of Atlanta, whose small investment in oil had turned into an income of $1,750 *per day*. After only forty days, the company began selling its second thousand set of lots. Notably, the names of the purchasers included no one from the Rawlings clan.[6]

---

[5] His business slogan of "You get the girl, we'll furnish the rest" apparently applied only to the furniture store, not to the funeral home.

[6] It is of note, however, that Mr. Beach's furniture store was located directly next to the Citizens Bank of Sandersville, both businesses in a building that was owned by Dr. William Rawlings and also housed the post office and part of the Rawlings Sanitarium.

Such promises of easy money were sure to arouse suspicion, as evidenced by an article in the June 12 *Atlanta Georgian* headlined, "Swindlers Are Running Riot Throughout the Nation Today." The reporter railed against the sale of "absolutely worthless" oil shares, declaring that "An ordinary band of card sharks, openly playing their game in every city, would do less harm and steal infinitely less money than is stolen by these promoters of fake oil schemes." The point could not have been more directly aimed at the new enterprise in Washington County.

Apparently unwilling to let any publicity—good or bad— go to waste, the promoters of the Middle Georgia Oil & Gas Company reproduced the article in full in their next week's ad, followed by the editorial comment, "To the above we heartily say—AMEN. The moral is deal with your own people and help with the development of your own state." They then went on to remind the public that their directors "are men whose integrity is undoubted, men who have been successful in business, whose patriotism and loyalty are unquestioned." It was unclear how their "patriotism and loyalty" might come into play in these particular transactions.

Sales of oil shares continued throughout the summer. By the time the offering was forty days old, more than a thousand units had been sold. With the arrival of the boll weevil in the county, the ads were changed to read, "The Most Effective and Quickest Fight You Can Make Is In Buying Washington County Oil and Gas Lots," adding, "it will only be a matter of a few months until our purchasers will forget Mr. Boll Weevil entirely."

The company planned to raise enough money to drill an exploratory well. By late August, sufficient funds had been acquired, and Professor Ross A. Craddock of San Antonio,

Texas, was hired as the "consulting geologist" who would pick the initial site for drilling. Professor Craddock discovered three additional sites of seepage and, more important, that a rod pushed down two or three feet in the sites and then withdrawn would release gas that could be ignited with "a blue flame flash," a sure sign that this had its origin in an oil deposit, not decaying vegetation. Craddock, described as "the best paid geologist in the country," announced, "I have never seen a more favorable condition or a more complete chain of evidence anywhere in all my experience as here. YOU WILL GET OIL and you will not only get it in your territory, but in other places. The site of the initial well having been set, the company offered a new series of shares for this particular location. The ads quoted an unnamed traveler who'd visited the property and said, "A man that will not buy this is mule-stubborn, closes his eyes, refuses to use his judgment and absolutely refuses to consider the future of his family."

While the Middle Georgia Oil & Gas Company had been selling shares since May, they seemed to have forgotten to register with the secretary of state's office, a necessary requirement for such enterprises. This precipitated both an investigation by the secretary's office and an examination of the site by State Geologist S. W. McCallie. At a hearing in Atlanta in early September, the company admitted that the lots, supposedly sufficient in size to sink an oil well, in fact measured twenty-five feet by twenty-five feet. Dr. McCallie had valued the company's 500-acre tract at $60 per acre; the prorated value of the lots being sold placed the value nearer $2,500 per acre. A compromise was reached in which it was decided that the Middle Georgia Oil & Gas Company was in fact selling "certificates of participation" rather than property or stock, and a generous refund policy was instituted.[7] Official permission to sell stock was granted on September 15.

With the legal niceties out of the way, the appeals to potential buyers became more strident. A new round of anecdotes of investors who had gotten rich in the oil fields of the West only reinforced the contention that this was one's "real opportunity to make a fortune…at home." Two girls— mere "library clerks" from Texas—had pooled their savings of $100, only to receive $1,200 a few months later. A man named Rowe from Louisiana had made seven million dollars in a single year. A derrick 110 feet high had been ordered, with plans to drill as deep as five thousand feet. It was only a matter of time. Citizens should "Get Ready for the Biggest Strike Georgia Has Ever Known."

As the year 1919 drew to a close, the company's ad pitches took aim at one group they may have missed, those who believed in divine intervention. With the pitch line, "Is The Hand of Providence Playing a Part in the Destiny of Our State?" they pointed out how Texas had been nearly struck down by years of drought, only to be rescued by the discovery of "oil everywhere, and the greatest prosperity ever known to any state." This happy ending for Georgia was sure to follow the completion of the initial exploratory well.

For those who might believe in prophecy and signs, however, there were other hints of things to come. In August, a seer named Professor Porta foresaw "a strange grouping of six mighty planets" destined to cause the "hugest biggest sunspot on record" to appear like "a vast wound in the side of the sun"

---

[7] The sale of the company's certificates, shares, lots, or "blue sky" (as the secretary of state termed it) was not limited to Washington County or even the state of Georgia. They were also registered as a corporation in South Carolina.

on December 17, 1919, or so reported the *Progress*. He predicted earthquakes, hurricanes, lightning, colossal rains, and volcanic eruptions. As if to reinforce his predictions, the heavens yielded further signs. In October, two comets were observed streaking their way across the night sky. In November, an eclipse of the sun darkened the heavens on an otherwise unremarkable Saturday morning in Sandersville. A few days later, a meteor "of tremendous size" plunged into Lake Michigan, causing a huge explosion and a pillar of fire that could be observed from as far as fifty miles away.

Meanwhile, in Washington County, life for Charlie Rawlings could not have been any better. An ad for the Citizens Bank reported the estimated worth of its stockholders (among whom he was the major one) as $2,500,000. Cotton prices closed for the year at an all-time high of nearly thirty-six cents a pound. The railroad, the warehouses, and his other agriculture-related businesses were thriving. Between him and his two brothers, all major landowners, the family controlled more than a hundred square miles of fertile Georgia cropland and timberland. In a further acknowledgment of the family's prominence (not to mention political clout), in late December, Mary Hardwick, daughter to now former senator and future governor Tom Hardwick, married Charlie's nephew. The prospects for the coming years seemed unlimited.

A few weeks later, a strange report appeared on the front page of the *Progress*:

> At the home of Mr. C. G. Rawlings in this city, last Thursday night, a large lump of coal was placed in the grate. It was only partially consumed by the fire. Friday morning when a fresh fire was being kindled the partially burned lump was broken up with a poker and a pair of scissors was found firmly embedded in it. The scissors were about eight inches long.

Clinging to them as if welded was a strip of slate which is usually found in coal mines. Mr. Rawlings states he is sure the scissors were not accidentally dropped in the grate, but came in the coal. The mystery as to how they got there cannot be solved, as it is supposed by geologists that the deposits of coal that are dug from the earth have been there for thousands of years.

The date of the article was December 17, the date forewarned by Professor Porta. Perhaps, as events would later show, this was another omen. Charlie Rawlings should have taken heed.

15

What Goes Up Must Come Down

The history of the United States as an independent nation has been characterized by economic cycles, with ups following downs and booms following busts in an irregular but recurrent pattern. According to the National Bureau of Economic Research, the so-called Great Recession of 1920–1921 officially began in January 1920 and ended some eighteen months later in August of the following year. By definition, such determinations are made retrospectively, as the data on which they are based are often slow in their collation and analysis and are based on trends rather than short-term deviations of the longer cycles.

The Great Recession was unique in several respects. It followed the greatest period of inflation in American history and was characterized by the sharpest one-year deflation since the beginning of the republic, exceeding even that of the later Great Depression of the 1930s.[1] Despite sharp swings in monetary value, gross national product, and employment rates, it was unusually short and followed by a rapid rebound of the national economy leading into the era of "The Roaring Twenties." While its effects were felt generally across the nation, they were not of equal severity in all economic sectors or geographic areas. Agriculture was particularly hard hit, with the following years characterized by falling farm income and land values, and a dramatic increase in farm foreclosures.

---

[1] Vernon 1991.

For small-town Georgia, the Great Recession was a death knell, heralding an era of decline and socioeconomic change that would last not for years but for decades. It marked the end of a golden era and the acceleration of a fundamental shift in the characteristics that had defined the state since its creation nearly a century and a half earlier. While some may have sensed that the good times could not last forever, the general mood in rural Georgia pointed toward business as usual. Cotton prices in 1919 had closed the year at an all-time high. Banks and merchants were thriving, their income fueled by the diffusion of growing wealth through local economies. Land prices had skyrocketed, land being the ultimate source of the prosperity that had swept across the countryside. W. J. Cash's description of the mood is appropriate:

> Here at length was the old dream apparently coming true: here was cotton sweeping toward a price of forty cents with such celerity that the soberest and most cautious traders began to talk of fifty cents, and the more excitable sort of a dollar. And so, throughout the South, in the towns, in the countryside, men—virtually all men who had money, who could borrow, or who could get credit—began to engage in a scramble to buy land; to buy it for all sorts of reasons, but above all because they confidently expected to sell it again tomorrow for a thumping profit. At the peak, in 1919 and 1920, I myself saw lands that had sold for two dollars an acre in the first years of the century fetch three hundred dollars.[2]

Not only did the land give life to cotton; there were also sure signs of vast treasures beneath it, mere hints of more riches to come. The year's inaugural issue of the *Sandersville Progress* announced that drilling for oil would begin soon. The site of the oil find, some twelve miles west of the city, had

---

[2] Cash 1941, 279.

become known as "the Beach field," for W. R. Beach on whose land the seepage was found. He confidently predicted, "If oil is developed Washington County will become one of the richest sections in the southern states and our towns and villages will increase in population to an astonishing degree." The drumbeat of weekly hard-sell ads accompanied by carefully crafted front-page news stories continued.

Charlie Rawlings's bank again declared a "fine dividend" of 12 percent as it had in years past, but with the footnote that higher expenses were more than offset by the increased demand for loans. Its ads touted "Resources" of $350,000 and again reminded current and potential depositors that its stockholders had an "Estimated Worth" of $2,500,000, the figures being given to "assure you safety" in banking with the institution. In mid-April, as cotton traded near an all-time high, Charlie's nineteen-year-old daughter Susan married William Arthur Wray, an up-and-coming young man who no doubt considered himself fortunate to have become a member of such a prominent and wealthy family.

Meanwhile, the Eighteenth Amendment ushered in Prohibition on January 17, its advent publicly celebrated by the Women's Christian Temperance Union and Ku Klux Klan alike, while privately ignored by most. The revived Klan, in early 1920 barely four years old and still a relatively small Georgia-based secret society, had yet to explode on the national scene. Its espoused goals of old-time moral values meshed closely with those of the ladies of the WCTU, reflecting the shift to conservatism in the early years following the Great War.

While the sun still rose in the east and set in the west, while the seasons still came and went with exacting regularity, there were abundant warnings of changes ahead for those who chose to see them. A local news piece from late December 1919 noted that the overall cost of living had risen 82.2 percent in the preceding five years, with food costs up 92 percent and clothing 135 percent. Inflation for the year had exceeded 15 percent and would exceed even this figure by the end of 1920.

On a national level, economists were alarmed at inflation's devaluation of the dollar. With the United States effectively off the gold standard since the creation of the Federal Reserve System, the expansion of the money supply and easing of credit that accompanied the war years had wreaked plenty of damage. Political winds shifted to reflect the growing consensus that the strength of the greenback must be restored. Some of the steps perceived necessary were already in place. Maximal marginal income tax rates, which stood at 7 percent in 1914, had been raised to a near-confiscatory level of 77 percent by 1918, dropping only slightly to 73 percent by 1919. These tax increases were deemed necessary to fund the war, but they remained in place after the war's end. The Federal Reserve stepped in by increasing discount rates to a peak of 7 percent in June 1920, a level unparalleled until the 1970s. Overall, these financial moves had the desired effect of reducing the availability of credit, the lifeblood of agriculture, and the fuel that powered speculation.

Warren Harding, who was to win the presidency on the Republican ticket in 1920, campaigned in part on the restoration of the value of the dollar. He railed against the policies of the Wilson administration, stating in his nomination acceptance speech, "Deflation on one hand and restoration of the 100 cent dollar on the other ought to have begun the day after the armistice, but plans were lacking or courage failed...." He was elected with the largest popular vote in American history up to that time. In his inaugural address, he promised "readjustment," noting that "the penalties will not be light, or evenly distributed." As president, he slashed government spending, reduced marginal tax rates, pressured the Federal Reserve to lower discount rates, and began a substantial reduction of the national debt. By mid-1921, the national economy had begun a robust recovery. But in the rural South, things were only beginning to get worse.

For the first months of 1920, it seemed as if Washington County might escape the economic downturn that was beginning to affect the rest of the nation. Cotton prices remained high, as did demand. In February, the Department of Commerce reported record cotton exports to Europe for the preceding month. By mid-spring, the futures market offered a bright picture also, with December cotton trading near thirty-five cents a pound. As the planting season began, the state Department of Agriculture reported with certainty that calcium arsenate, when used properly, was a successful and effective way of controlling the boll weevil. Equally important, control could be achieved at a cost that still allowed a reasonable profit—with the understood assumption, of course, that cotton prices stayed in the same general range.

In the Beach oil field, the news was positive as well. Drilling had begun and shares[3] were being sold at a rate of nearly a thousand a week, if the company's ads were to be believed. Gatherings and barbecues were held, addressed by motivational speakers, where the idiocy of failing to buy an interest was driven home with all the zeal of an old-fashioned

---

[3] It is somewhat unclear exactly what the Middle Georgia Oil & Gas Company was selling. The ads and articles variously refer to the certificates of participation sold to investors as shares, units, or lots. If the press and publicity were accurate, however, each purchase was almost certainly a ticket to riches.

tent revival. An extended payment plan was available for as little as five dollars per month if three or more lots were purchased. As one orator pointed out, the cost of a single lot was scarcely more than "an ordinary evening's entertainment," and the risk no more "than you'd lose if you bought a hog that died." As an additional benefit, the drill bit plunging into the fertile middle Georgia soil had found "valuable deposits" of bauxite and "snow white clay," the latter worth "twelve to fifteen dollars per ton."

The slow drip of bad news and disaster began mid-spring. On May 19, J. E. Johnson, the Citizens Bank's cashier, the Sandersville Railroad's vice president, and the close friend, confidant, and fellow investor of Charlie Rawlings, dropped dead at a banker's meeting at the Dempsey Hotel in Macon. As head cashier, he had been in charge of day-to-day operation of the bank. His unexpected death left a void not only in the bank's management but also in the support, advice, and counsel he offered his employer and mentor. The head bookkeeper was elevated to the position of cashier, but the guidance, experience, and wisdom of Johnson would be sorely missed, as subsequent events would reveal.

The boll weevil appeared in the county in late May, and by mid-June it was said to be "found in large numbers in every field of cotton," as "thick as flies." Some farmers were using calcium arsenate, while others used patented weevil traps or resorted to having their workers pick off the pests by hand. The outlook for the crop was said to be "not at all promising."

The ripple effect of the dire outlook and the tightening of credit began to spread throughout the state and local economy. State revenues plummeted. The governor had reached the legal limit of his borrowing power, and after the payment on the state's bonded indebtedness due July 1, the treasury would be left with only $8,842. It was hoped that insurance taxes would help tide the state over until income picked up. One of Sandersville's most prominent merchants announced that because of bad accounts, he was adopting a policy of "Sell for cash and sell for less." For an economy that had depended almost entirely on credit for decades, this was a dramatic change. The local paper echoed the sentiment with an editorial urging customers to pay all bills promptly or, better, to pay on the spot with cash.

For the first time, the boll weevil did serious damage to the county's cotton production. With the early harvest, it was estimated that the cotton crop would be only one-third of its usual size. Cotton prices inexplicably began a downhill slide. One estimate in mid-September held that the average farmer would lose five hundred dollars "for each plow," but this was when cotton was still bringing about thirty cents a pound. For men like Charlie Rawlings who operated six hundred plows, the loss would be devastating, but the news only got worse. With ever-accelerating speed, cotton prices fell, closing the year at less than twelve cents a pound, with the outlook for 1921 even bleaker.

As cash dried up, merchants who had once dealt almost entirely on credit sales saw their incomes slashed. With the crash in cotton prices, buyers hoarded what little cash they had, fearful of taking on any debt they might not be able to repay. One storeowner announced that he would accept cotton in payment of accounts due or in exchange at a fixed rate for merchandise in stock.

The American Cotton Association blamed the fall in prices on "organized bearish" speculators and called for farmers to hold their cotton off the market in warehouses until a reasonable price could be reestablished. While blamed on speculation, it is likely that a decrease in demand was the prime factor in the declining value. In a further effort to suppress cotton production, gin owners were pressured to temporarily shut down their ginneries, hoping the decrease in supply would serve to increase prices. The notices sometimes came as warnings posted on the gin's door and at other times were delivered in person by masked men in the regalia of the Knights of the Ku Klux Klan. The Imperial Wizard denied responsibility for these "night riders" and called for their apprehension.

This lack of demand affected not only cotton but also cottonseed oil, a major secondary source of farm income. In Macon, two of the city's five cotton oil mills closed in early October, citing farmers' refusal to accept a price for seed that was half of what it had been a year earlier. Even the oil, which in better days had sold for twenty to twenty-two cents a pound, found no takers when offered at eight cents a pound.

While some cotton gin fires may have been started by masked men resembling members of the Klan, insurance companies reported a rash of automobiles being burned for the insurance proceeds. The *Augusta Chronicle* quoted an insurance agent who said he knew "quite a number of the large [insurance] companies are seriously considering withdrawing from the automobile insurance business in the south."

Among the mainstays of the small-town business community, perhaps hardest hit were the banks. Loosely regulated, they were the source of funds for merchants and farmers, not to mention those who saw land as a "good investment" to be purchased with borrowed funds. The bank failure rate rose rapidly in the early 1920s as borrowers were increasingly unable to pay their debts. On Sunday evening, October 3, 1920, J. H. Arnold, cashier of the Tennille Banking Company and major stockholder of the Bank of Harrison, a small crossroads bank some ten miles to the southeast, was found inside the vault of the Tennille bank, having shot himself in the temple with a pistol. Both banks[4] faced the loss of "considerable sums" due to the bankruptcy of a large account, and it was initially thought that Arnold's suicide resulted from his concern over this. The bank's directors felt obligated to post a large notice on the front page of the paper assuring depositors of the bank's soundness and the absence of "any shortage or irregularity whatever," attributing Arnold's death to "a fit of gloom" brought on by family concerns.

As to the Citizens Bank of Sandersville, the outlook by the end of the year had turned from one of prosperity to one of uncertainty. Total deposits were less than half what they had been a year earlier, but total loan volume remained about the same. The money out on loan now represented more than twice the bank's total deposits. To cover the difference, the bank was forced to borrow from other banks, just at the time when the inter-bank lending rate was at a historic high. The decision to make "long term loans" against land had never anticipated the current situation.

By year's end, the county's coffers were also running dry. The tax collector reported "that there is not enough cash coming in to meet everyday expenses," and the Board of Roads and Revenues was unable to find even temporary financing. Landowners were not only unable to pay their property taxes but their amounts due would also be increasing by 75 percent because of the assessed increase in real-estate values.

---

[4] The Bank of Harrison would fail within the decade. The Tennille Banking Company would survive this crisis only to fail some six decades later.

The downturn had produced some limited good news. By the end of the year, local prices were beginning to drop. Sugar was selling for less than half the price of a year earlier, and there were significant declines in flour and other food products. Inflation, which had peaked at an annualized rate of nearly 24 percent in June 1920, had fallen to less than 3 percent by December and would enter deflationary territory in the new year. Also, the migration of black farm workers to northern cities had dramatically lessened, the need obviated by the labor pool of returning American troops and the general economic contraction caused by the recession.

The one bright light at the end of the tunnel seemed to be Washington County's oil discovery. The huge derrick, surrounded by wooden shacks and towering over a blighted field of stumps and broken trees, had been christened the "Lillian B. No. 1" by Mrs. W. L. Williams, wife of the owner of the local Coca-Cola Bottling Company, who was also one of the directors. Drilling advanced slowly, as more and more lots were sold. By mid-April, the company had opened a sales office in Columbia, South Carolina, announcing its intention to obtain oil leases in other promising areas in Georgia and adjacent states. It hoped to have 100,000 acres under lease by September 1.

In late spring 1920, the company expanded its operations nearly a hundred miles south to Jeff Davis County, Georgia, banking on completing a failed oil exploration project that had sunk a well some 900 feet in 1908. The original well had supposedly shown positive signs of oil before the project was scuttled due to some alleged disagreement among the owners. The main evidence for oil's presence there was the memory of one of the drillers, John A. Chromartie. While Mr. Chromartie

Promising vast riches from the sure-to-be-discovered pool of oil that lay hidden beneath the earth of Washington County, the Middle Georgia Oil & Gas Company drilled into the earth as well as the pockets of gullible investors.

was quite specific in his memory of the details of the well, all the data, including the well log and analysis of specimens, had been destroyed in a fire some years earlier. Further support was obtained through affidavits of acknowledgment (if not support) from a "Geologist of National Reputation," as well as the state geologist and the secretary of state. This well was to be christened "The Lillian B. No. 2."

By late August, the slogan was "Oil by Christmas" with dividends by the end of the year, a mere four months away. By mid-September, the Lillian B. No. 1 had reached a depth of only about 400 feet despite six months of drilling. The Lillian B. No. 2 in Jeff Davis County was planning to start with a double shift of workers, and after only two weeks of drilling showed faint but unmistakable signs of oil. Even though the company had been in business now for a year and a third, ads reminded potential investors that it was still possible to "get in on the ground floor."

By early December, the Lillian B. No. 1, now called "The Old Mother," had only reached a depth of 426 feet, essentially the same level of three months earlier. News reports attributed the delay to a breakage of the drill linkage, but the driller, "working eighteen to twenty-four hours" a day, had managed to fix the problem and drilling was to resume. Ads noted, "White Lightning is barred from the camp. You can expect some quick and efficient work in Number One from now on." The oil company's sales manager, Charles Peeler, announced that he only had "a few more shares to sell" and was moving the company's headquarters to a hotel room in Sandersville, ostensibly to remain close to the action and accommodate the many shareholders who wanted to visit the project.

At year's end, the greatest hope on the horizon was the prospect of discovering the "vast pool of oil" that surely lay hidden beneath Washington County's cotton fields. But, as with the state of the economy in general, there was ample evidence of a not-so-certain future. In late 1919, Dr. McCallie and two assistant state geologists had released a brief report[5] on the prospect of oil being found in Telfair County, not far from the Middle Georgia Oil & Gas Company's Lillian B. No. 2 well. The report reminded readers, "It is very seldom that conditions indicating commercial oil bodies are shown by surface phenomena, consequently not too much confidence should be placed in...oil seeps." With an abundance of caution, Dr. McCallie concluded, "In putting down test wells in...unproved areas, it should be fully understood by the citizens of the State that the undertaking is a gamble pure and simple with the chances of winning small." He had apparently neglected to read the ads of the Middle Georgia Oil & Gas Company.

---

[5] S. W. McCallie 1919.

16

The Wrath of God and Man

If things had seemed bad in 1920, they were only destined to become worse the following year. The year-end Southern Cotton Conference in Memphis had unanimously agreed that a 50 percent reduction in total yield for the 1921 crop was necessary if prices were to be restored to profitable levels. Enlisting merchants and bankers as "strong advocates and willing helpers," the trade group demanded enforcement through "credit restriction and denial of credit to any planter or farmer or supply merchant or landowner who will not comply with the reduction plan." On a state level, Governor Dorsey designated February 10 as "Cotton Acreage Reduction Day." Even the local grand jury joined the chorus, calling for "a radical curtailment of the cotton acreage for 1921." In Washington County, though, they need not have bothered; the boll weevil had already done the job for them. The final ginning report indicated that the county had produced about 12,000 bales for the 1920 season, a bit less than half the usual crop.

Not to be seen as uncooperative, the Citizens Bank ran a vaguely threatening ad stating, "We cannot promise you, even if you do reduce the acreage, that you will get more money for your cotton than you are getting now, however we do promise you that if you grow cotton without growing food for men and feed for animals, we will all be worse off than bankrupt." In fact, it is likely that the bank had little money to loan anyway. At the start of the new year, nearly half of their outstanding loans were funded by money borrowed from other banks.

Many were uncollectible. Deposits continued to plummet as cash flow dried up across the local economy at large. For the first time in a number of years, the bank failed to announce a dividend.

The warehouses were full of cotton as farmers held out for a turn in the market. In early February, Charlie Rawlings sold 500 bales at 11.75 cents a pound, commenting that "he had become tired out with watchful waiting" and decided to convert the remainder of his 1920 cotton to cash. It was a horribly low price but better than the 9.4 cents he would have gotten if he'd held on until April or May. Worse, due to inflation, the $29,375 he received would buy only a fraction of what it would have bought five years earlier.

In the biblical book of Exodus, it is recounted that Yahweh, God of the Israelites, visited upon the pharaoh and the Egyptian people a series of plagues to demonstrate his power and to punish them for their captivity of his chosen people. The arrival of the boll weevil and the events of 1920 had led some ministers to suggest that perhaps God was trying to send a similar message to America of the twentieth century. The clear decline in the old morality, the open flaunting of intoxicating liquors in the day of national Prohibition, the telephone, the radio, and the increasing tendency of young people to engage in unchaperoned dating all pointed to the conclusion that the nation was on the road to destruction. If such were the case, and God were indeed angry, he would amply demonstrate his displeasure over a long weekend in February.

February 10 had been a day of heavy thunderstorms, unusual for mid-winter in Georgia. Near noon, the rain ceased for a few moments to be replaced by a menacing black cloud that hovered over the hamlet of Oconee, about eight miles south of where the Lillian B. No. 1 was punching her way into the earth. A whirlwind emerged from the cloud to descend on an area of small homes where many families were enjoying their midday meal. More than forty tenant houses were destroyed, leaving the ground as clean as if it had been "swept by a giant broom." The twister then attacked the local white schoolhouse, a newly built wood-frame structure, lifting the roof and sending the walls crashing in on seventy-five children. Miraculously, no one was killed as a quick-thinking teacher had instructed them to take cover under their desks.[1]

Having done its work in the village, the tornado skipped off across the countryside to damage several outlying farms. By the end of the day, the bodies of twenty-three negroes and one "white lad" had been found, some having been carried as far as half a mile away by the winds. Initial reports said at least twelve people were still missing, with the death toll expected to rise.

Less than three days later, nature's wrath was visited upon Sandersville. At 5:30 AM on a quiet Sunday morning after the night marshal had gone home to bed, a lightning strike torched the row of buildings that bordered the west side of the City Square, spreading rapidly to the venerable Mason Temple Building. Attempts were made to contain the flames, but the rotting water hose burst, and even when a new hose was procured, the water pressure was so low that little could be done. By midmorning, it all lay in ruins.

If anything, the Masonic Temple was the city's greatest pride, a living link to its past and a proud showcase that dated from the 1850s, the previous Golden Age of Cotton. Con-

---

[1] Free-range animals were not so fortunate, however, as newspaper reports noted that, "Several pigs under the building were killed instantly" (*Sandersville Progress*, 16 February 1921).

figured in the form of a Greek temple and constructed by slaves, its fluted Ionic columns were fashioned from hand-formed bricks and topped by carved stone scrolls. It was the one building on the square that had been spared Sherman's torch, the courthouse and other structures having all been burned in November 1864. For intrepid travelers willing to brave the muddy Dixie Highway, it was a popular tourist attraction.

But the fire had destroyed more than a simple building. The Masonic meeting room, accessed by a side door, was upstairs. The ground floor held the city's only library, a collection of more than 7,000 volumes, plus a museum housing irreplaceable relics from the county's early history dating back to the Revolutionary War.

As the walls of the now-destroyed building were being pulled down, a hollow, hewn granite cornerstone was discovered concealed in the northeast corner. It was considered a fortuitous find; there had been no external indication that it was there. Under the stone, hidden from view for nearly sixty-five years, was a marble slab bearing the date December 27, 1856. Inside the cornerstone was a sealed copper box. The discovery of this time capsule was a topic of great curiosity, and its formal opening was scheduled to be held at a courthouse ceremony on February 23. Inside the box were two coins, Masonic memorabilia, and several newspapers, the latter so badly decomposed as to be almost unreadable. The one thing that could still be seen, however, was the price paid for cotton at the end of the season in 1856. It was trading at 11.75 to 12 cents a pound, almost precisely what it was trading for in

The venerable 'Masonic Temple' Building, constructed in 1856 of slave-made bricks and the only structure on Sandersville's City Square spared by General Sherman, burned to the ground after from a lightning-caused fire in February 1921.

1921. When corrected for inflation, cotton's value had fallen to a mere fraction of what it had been two-thirds of a century earlier. The message seemed clear.

The Citizens Bank's ads took on a humbler tone, referring to "these times of readjustment and temporary depression." Gone were the days of boasting of the worth of its stockholders. Now the theme was one of shared suffering and "pulling together." "Take Losses and Forget Them." "The Quitter Always Loses." "Grit Your Teeth and Let's Go," and, by the way, "Your Account Will Be Appreciated." The new motto was "Prompt, Progressive, Polite."

The outlook for the coming crop season was dismal. The normally brisk demand for mules had evaporated. In good years, a hundred train carloads or more would be sold. By mid-March not a single load had been shipped in, with the main trade being animals that were coming back on the market as farmers curtailed their operations. The story was the same with fertilizer. Normally hundreds of carloads would have been sold. In this doubtful spring of 1921, estimates were "only two or three."

In late April, there was a report of a positive move in the economy. It was announced that C. G. Rawlings had purchased all of the shares of the Sandersville Oil Mill, one of the two cottonseed oil production facilities in the county. He already owned about three-quarters of the stock, and with his purchase of the remainder from his first cousin Ben Tarbutton, he gained complete control. He immediately transferred the shares to his new son-in-law, W. A. Wray, retaining the $25,000 worth of outstanding bonds for himself. The move would seem to indicate that at least one knowledgeable businessman expected the cotton market to improve. The *Progress* commented that "Mr. Rawlings, who is one of the largest landowners in Middle

Georgia, produces several hundred bales of cotton annually and he will grow enough cotton seed to keep the mill running several weeks without buying seed in the open market."

Others seemed to be counting on the improvement of the economy also. In May, the Atlanta Cadillac Company's new building and showroom was formally opened with a gala reception followed by a dinner for more than a hundred guests at the Georgian Terrace Hotel. Because the company was the major Cadillac dealer in the southeast, the festivities attracted "powerful men in the automobile and financial fields" from as far away as New York and Detroit. The "Sandersville Boys" were on a roll. Locally, the Masons announced ambitious plans for a "thoroughly modern" three-story building to be built on the site of the ruined temple.

Meanwhile, the Middle Georgia Oil & Gas Company was on the cusp of great discoveries with its wells in Washington and Jeff Davis counties. In January, it was said to be "only a matter of days" before oil was found. In February, there was assurance that the Lillian B. No. 1 "may strike [a] gusher almost any day." Newspaper reports—thinly disguised adver-tisements, really—gushed themselves:

> When the drill strikes the expected gusher there will be a stampede of people from everywhere to this point and there will be such a development in business that no one can predict how many millionaires will be created by the dormant wealth of Washington County which has been hidden under the ground for all of these years. It will be like rubbing Aladdin's lamp for the creation of wealth, as it will come with a gush. People will then forget there is such a thing as the boll weevil evil.

The ads, meanwhile, reminded investors that stock was still available.

In March, under a headline of "The Oil and Gas May Come to Pass,"[2] it was reported that several geologists from Louisiana and Texas had spent six weeks studying the potential oil field in Jeff Davis County and were "very optimistic." The well was now reported to be at a depth of 1,400 feet. A letter from Dr. McCallie, the state geologist, reviewed the soil data from the well log, none of which suggested formations associated with oil. W. R. Beach, the company's president, explained this by noting that "Dr. McCallie is very cautious, as he should be, in giving out this information as he is representing the state at large and should there be a failure he would be criticized for same. I think if you will write the Doctor a letter, you can get at first hand just what our prospects are." Drilling—as well as sales of shares—continued.

At three o'clock on Friday morning, May 20, the town was awakened by a "spectacular blaze" at the Sandersville Oil Mill. Exactly four weeks had elapsed since Charlie Rawlings had purchased the remaining stock and transferred it to his son-in-law. "Those who were first on the scene stated the fire seemed to be raging in several different places." And to make matters worse, there were a number of explosions that were attributed to dynamite stored in the mill. All buildings were a total loss. The mill's destruction was a major blow to the community. Other than a small millwork plant, it was "the only manufacturing establishment in the city," with a payroll of about seven hundred dollars per week. Fortunately there was insurance to cover at least part of the loss. There was no word initially as to whether or not there were plans to rebuild.

As spring melted into summer, the boll weevil reemerged in a major way. Once again, weevils were reported "as thick as

---

[2] It is unclear whether the pun was deliberate or accidental.

flies in the cotton fields," but "in much larger numbers" than in previous years. Early reports indicated that although calcium arsenate might be effective, the "applications are expensive, and a large majority of our farmers will not take the risk." They were willing to take their chances with God and nature.

While the prospects of a successful cotton crop seemed remote, an ad placed by the Citizens Bank in July announced "A New Mill Is Being Built," commenting, "This mill is one that grinds slow but grinds exceedingly fine." Readers were invited to see the next week's paper for more details. The following week, the bank's ad stated that the new mill, now dubbed "The Money Mill," was selling stock. It was guaranteed to pay a non-cash dividend of 4 percent per year, in addition to a share of any profits.

Whether or not the stock issue was successful is not known, as three weeks later it was announced that the fire that destroyed the Sandersville Oil Mill in May was the result of arson. The night watchman, seventy-two-year-old H. T. Brown, had been arrested and "made a full confession, implicating others in the plot." Nothing more was heard of the new "Money Mill."

While the "others" who might be involved in the torching of the mill were not named, there was one person who clearly stood to profit by it. Charlie surely had purchased the remaining interest in the mill at a bargain price. Cotton production was off sharply, and cottonseed oil, formerly a lucrative byproduct, had become almost unsalable for any decent price. The county had one other cotton oil mill in Tennille. At this point it wasn't clear that there was need for a second facility. The one thing of value the mill did possess, however, was insurance coverage. This would have been taken out in the glory days of the past when the processing of cottonseed was a lucrative enterprise. As a going concern, the actual value of the mill was dubious. As the subject of an insurance settlement, however, it was a sure thing. Sure enough to make someone want to store dynamite in an oil mill. Even in the Dog Days of summer, the wheels of justice, like those of the proposed "Money Mill," were grinding slowly but grinding exceedingly fine.

17

The Chickens Come Home to Roost

By August 1921, it was evident that the year's cotton was, for practical purposes, lost. Boll weevil infestation was described as "heavy on all the farms," and the expectations called for an "exceedingly short" crop. By late summer and early fall as the cotton crop trickled in, the predictions of dire losses were confirmed. The county, which formerly had a large number of operating ginneries, was now down to one, and estimates were that the crop seemed to be about one-seventh of its normal output. A writer commented in the *Progress*, "This is the hardest year since the boll weevil appeared, as no one has made enough to pay expenses of cultivation, and consequently there is but little money in circulation." The domino effect had clearly affected the bankers and merchants and had also spread to the labor market. The paper reported, "There is no demand for labor and many who have been dependant on farm work for a living are standing idle with no prospects of employment." For those who were able and willing, there seemed little choice but to pack up and try to survive elsewhere, far from the fields of cotton.

Perhaps hoping that bravado would change the outlook, the Citizens Bank ran a boldly lettered quarter-page ad announcing "One Million Dollars to Loan to the Farmers on Cotton." It was a strange proposition. Deposits were down to less than 20 percent of what they had been two years earlier, and by year's end outstanding loans would equal more than 400 percent of total deposits. There was no money to loan.

To make matters worse, the September session of the local grand jury announced the indictments of C. G. Rawlings, H. T. Brown, and four blacks, including Charlie's driver Hal Hooks, on a charge of arson in the burning of the oil mill in May. Although the indictments were not unexpected, the plan had been to keep them secret until the last minute and then proceed immediately to trial. It was well recognized that any undue delay between the bringing of formal charges and the trial would give the defendants time to buy a few jurors. In order to avoid the chance of Rawlings and the other defendants convincing Brown to recant his confession, he was arrested and placed in jail to be held until the trial could get underway. Charlie posted bond without having to appear in court. When the state's plans were thwarted "on account of sickness and absence of some of the lawyers retained for the defense," it became necessary to postpone the case until the March 1922 term of court.

The devastated economy had begun to affect even the sentencing of criminals. Albert Howard, a man charged with killing his wife[1] earlier in the summer, faced a jury of his peers in the September term of Superior Court. He was quickly convicted and normally would have been sentenced to hang. The jury reasoned, however, that it would be to the county's advantage to sentence him to life in prison. They "argued that it would cost the county fifty dollars to hang and bury him, while his services to the county [as convict labor] would be worth three hundred dollars a year with an expectancy of twenty years of labor, making a total of $6,000." At least one man could give thanks for hard times.

Charlie Rawlings had not only become the target of the state court system but his farming activities had also drawn

---

[1] The local paper used the proper term "uxoricide."

federal scrutiny. At 5:30 PM on May 3, 1921, a letter[2] was mailed from the Sandersville Post Office addressed simply to "Attorney General, United States, Washington, D.C." Inside was a crudely written and unsigned note stating, "Investigate please C. G. Rawlings of this city for Peonage on his large farm in Johnson Co. Ga. near Bartow Ga. Send a good niger [sic] detective. One that is OK." Peonage, involuntary servitude, had become a significant political issue as farmers, landowners, and others attempted to stem the tide of southern blacks migrating to the North. The report was duly assigned a case number, and a letter was dispatched to the local Department of Justice office in Atlanta with instructions to "give this matter appropriate attention."

The author of the letter clearly wanted to remain anonymous. The script was crude and labored, and the handwritten address on the exterior of the envelope was penned in a different and more experienced style. For a large planter like Charlie, the loss of farm labor could be disastrous, and in many ways it represented as much of a threat as the boll weevil. Extreme measures were often taken, frequently with the cooperation of local law enforcement officials. Since many, perhaps most, of those attempting to leave were sharecroppers, it was relatively easy to claim that departure during the crop year represented the violation of some contract between the landowner and 'cropper, or that there were credit purchases advanced that must be repaid in full before the tenant would be allowed to leave. As the entire sharecropping system was based in large part on credit and future earnings, such charges were easily made and quickly enforced by local magistrates.

---

[2] Anonymous 1921.

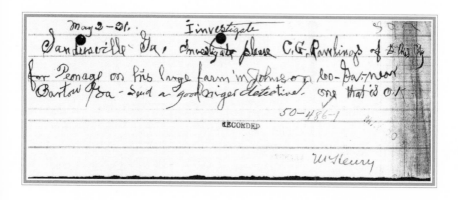

This crudely written note was delivered to the United States Attorney General in Washington in May 1921. It reads, "Investigate please C. G. Rawlings of this city for Peonage on his large farm in Johnson Co. Ga. near Bartow Ga. Send a good niger [sic] detective. One that is OK."

The nature of Charlie Rawlings's alleged offense of peonage will never be known. For a man so well connected, a few well-placed words and perhaps a few dollars changing hands was all that was necessary. It is important to note that his attorney and friend, Tom Hardwick, had won the gubernatorial election of 1920, becoming Georgia's governor in June 1921. The matter of peonage disappeared, having been given "appropriate attention."

Even as the national economy began to improve in late 1921, farmers and residents of Georgia's small towns were often driven to desperate measures. Prohibition had done little to dent the demand for now-illegal liquor; scarcely a week went by without news of the sheriff destroying yet another liquor still. Fires at insured homes and businesses were common. The local postal clerk in charge of COD packages was charged with embezzlement, despite his generous salary of $150 per month. The shipping agent for the Sandersville Railroad was arrested after more than $2,000 was found to be missing.

For those who had been holding out for the riches of the "vast pool of oil" that was sure to lie hidden under Washington County, their hopes were dashed in early September when W. R. Beach, president of the Middle Georgia Oil & Gas Company, sent a letter to those who had invested in its shares. "We very much regret to inform you…," the letter began, going on to say that it had been necessary to suspend drilling operations "on account of the financial depression," as well as "a malaria epidemic among our drilling crew," the latter excuse sounding as improbable as the existence of oil in the first place. Beach stated that he hoped to resume drilling at some point in the future, but nothing more was heard of him or the entire enterprise.[3]

Since spring 1921, Charlie's older brother Ben had been plagued by weight loss and abdominal pain. He had been finishing out a long and distinguished career as an attorney, legislator, and Superior Court judge, planning to practice a bit of law and attend to his extensive farming interests. Widowed after twenty-seven years of marriage, he had remarried in 1917 to his law partner's sister, a woman exactly half his age. His hopes of spending his dotage with his new wife and their young son,[4] by 1921 a three-year-old toddler, were destroyed when his symptoms were found to be due to the diagnosis of "stomach cancer." When journeys to national medical centers in Baltimore and New York confirmed that no effective treatment was available, Ben Rawlings returned home to prepare for his impending death.

Like many well-to-do small-town professionals of the area, Ben was extensively involved in cotton farming, owning between 12,000 and 15,000 acres of land near and around Sandersville. And, as with many others across the economic spectrum, the crash in cotton prices had caught him unawares. While he had significant assets, he was heavily involved in farming and therefore carried significant debts.

The Rawlings siblings' father, Frederick, had lived to the ripe old age of ninety, spending his final years in the home of his son and daughter-in-law, Charlie and Lula. When his father died in fall 1912, Charlie had assumed control of the personal property in the estate, eventually planning to distribute it

---

[3] For additional information on efforts to find oil in Georgia, please see the "Chapter Notes" section near the end of the book.

[4] The author's father—William Rawlings, Sr.

among the rightful heirs. Or so it was said. Years passed and nothing was done.

By fall 1921, Ben lay dying in his brother William's hospital, determined to settle this one issue while he was still alive. Charlie was summoned to his bedside, and both of his brothers confronted him with the fact that he had refused to divide the estate among its heirs. Charlie responded, "Well, Ben, I'll get up my papers and figgers and come and have a settlement with you and Doc."[5] Ben reminded Charlie that he'd been saying the same thing for years and that they intended to sue him. Charlie responded, "If you feel that way about it go ahead." And they did. Ben died in late November, but not before giving depositions and ensuring that his heirs would pursue the case.

The lawsuit dragged on for a year and was eventually settled for $10,318.46, plus $1,200 in attorney's fees. In lieu of cash, Ben's estate was paid with stock in the Davisboro Cotton Warehouse Company, The Farmers Gin Company, The Citizens Bank of Sandersville, Warehouse and Realty Corporation, and eighty shares in the Sandersville Railroad. His brother William forgave his portion.

Charlie was now a broken man. At age sixty-three, he was under indictment for arson and under investigation for involuntary servitude of his farm workers. He was deeply, perhaps terminally, in debt. His bank, the pride of his possessions, was failing. His own brothers were suing him. With his assets and income inextricably linked to the cotton economy, the outlook was grim.

On Saturday night, December 10, 1921, Charlie's wife of thirty-three years died suddenly and unexpectedly. Lula was fifty-one years old and, as far as everyone knew, was said to be

---

[5] Wood 1971.

in good health. It was reported that she had taken a short walk in the cool evening air, then returned home and suddenly collapsed, dying within minutes. Her front-page, praise-filled obituary attributed her death to "acute indigestion and heart failure," but the death certificate, the formal record of the cause of death, is less clear. It was signed by H. A. Hermann, MD, partner in practice with Dr. William Rawlings, Charlie's brother. Instead of listing a "Cause of Death" as required by law, Dr. Hermann wrote, "Was called Dec. 10, 7:30 PM. Found her dying. She expired in a few minutes."[6]

Beyond what the written record holds, any comments on the actual cause of Lula's death must necessarily fall in the realm of speculation. Even in 1921, however, the unexpected death of an otherwise healthy middle-aged woman was a legitimate cause for inquiry. The failure to list a cause of death on her death certificate is even more puzzling, leading to the possibility that she may have taken her own life. Rather than the member of a prominent Burke County family who married Charlie Rawlings, she had become "Mrs. C. G. Rawlings," the name listed on the certificate. As such, her husband's troubles were her troubles, and perhaps they were too much to face. The arson indictment, the lawsuit, and the thought of possible bankruptcy surely weighed heavily on her mind in the short, dark days of late fall 1921. But there may have been more, an event or revelation she simply could not face. While the exact timing of what happened is not known, Lula may have viewed Charlie's encounter with the Ku Klux Klan as the last straw.

---

[6] Public death certificate.

18

One Hundred Percent Americanism

Any discussion of Georgia in the 1920s would be incomplete without mention of the Ku Klux Klan. For much of the early part of the decade, it was a powerful and driving force in the politics and daily life not only of the state but also of the nation at large. As a social movement, it found fertile ground in the economically suffering villages and small towns of the cotton belt, electing officials, influencing law enforcement, and dispensing its own form of vigilante justice to an often-fearful populace. By 1930, the Klan had waned in power, destroyed by its own corruption and excesses but remembered for its violence and disdain for the rule of law.

It was perhaps inevitable that the paths of Charlie Rawlings and the Klan would intersect, and not necessarily in a good way. For Charlie Rawlings—prominent citizen, husband, father, bank president, and wealthy landowner—was also a noted philanderer. For that, the Klan had castrated him.

To the average American of the early twenty-first century, mention of the Ku Klux Klan evokes images of lynching and Southern racism. But the Klan, in its several incarnations, was far more complicated than that. W. J. Cash, in his introspective *The Mind of the South*, described the Klan during its heyday years of the 1920s as "an authentic folk movement."[1] It boasted of members in all forty-eight states, including many northern cities. By 1924, there were active Klaverns (local chapters) from

---

[1] Cash 1941, 335.

New England to California, with less than one-sixth of the national membership residing in the South.[2]

The Ku Klux Klan began in the Reconstruction South of 1865. Originally organized by Confederate veterans as a resistance movement to northern occupation and imposed Republican rule, it rapidly became a terrorist organization whose methods included intimidation, beatings, and murder. Its targets were freedmen, carpetbaggers, and politically active Republicans, with the goal being the suppression of black voting rights and restoration of the rule of the Democratic Party. Although former Confederate general Nathan Bedford Forrest became the first national Grand Wizard, the Klan had little formal organization, and most local chapters operated independently.

By 1869, the Klan's violence and excesses had perverted its original purpose, and Forrest ordered it disbanded. Given the lack of a formal hierarchal structure, many local chapters ignored the mandate. The Klan, or individuals representing themselves as members of the Klan, continued their paramilitary activities until finally suppressed by martial law, aggressive federal prosecution, and the eventual return of Democratic rule in the late 1870s. By 1880, the Klan had ceased to exist.

The Klan of the 1860s and 1870s would have been a mere footnote in history were it not for the vision of a failed Methodist minister named William J. Simmons. Simmons belonged to a dozen or more fraternal organizations and relished their secrecy and rituals of brotherhood. He envisioned a revived Ku Klux Klan, a secret fraternal order based on "one hundred percent Americanism," with respect for "old-time religion" and conventional moral authority. In practice, this meant

---

[2] Jackson 1967, 15.

aggressive disdain for negroes, Jews, Roman Catholics, and foreigners in general, not to mention disdain for extramarital sex and infidelity, bootlegging and alcoholism, nightclubs and bawdy houses, and dope.

In November 1915, Simmons launched his organization atop Stone Mountain near Atlanta in a nighttime ceremony illuminated by a burning cross. He then set out to spread his vision of a re-arisen Klan across the South. Despite more than four years of effort, by early 1920 Simmons had managed to recruit only a couple thousand members in Georgia and Alabama. The reincarnated Klan at the time "could best be described as just another indolent southern fraternal group"[3] not unlike the Knights of Pythias or the Mystic Shriners.

Simmons realized that he could not reach the full potential of his new organization on his own. In June 1920, he contracted with two Atlantans, Edward Young Clarke, the former newspaper reporter, and Mrs. Elizabeth Tyler, a divorcée of uncertain background, who together were in business under the name of the Southern Publicity Association. Clarke was the same journalist who in 1903 had written so glowingly of Washington County. He and Tyler had previously done promotional work for such organizations as the Red Cross and the Salvation Army, but they were willing to offer their services to Simmons if the price was right. It was; he agreed to give them 80 percent of the ten-dollar membership fee for each new Klansman they recruited. They launched a carefully planned membership drive.

The response exceeded Simmons's wildest dreams. Within a few months, the Klan's membership had soared to a hundred thousand. By September 1921, a *New York World* exposé of the Klan estimated its membership at half a million in forty-five

[3] Ibid., 7.

states. At the peak of its power in the mid-1920s, the Klan's membership was estimated to be between two and four million[4] individuals, with approximately half residing in urban areas throughout the United States.

Klan members, particularly early in its period of rapid expansion, were drawn from a broad range of society. Masonic lodges, given their tradition of secrecy and ritual, were ready sources of new members. Protestant clergy represented another large group, attracted by the Klan's emphasis on morality and religious observance. The individual makeup of Klaverns varied but often included professionals such as physicians and lawyers, as well as both skilled and blue-collar workers. As its strength and numbers grew, many politicians supported or joined—or at least didn't oppose—local Klan organizations.

Much of the rapid growth of the Klan in the early 1920s can be understood in the context of the social changes that were taking place across America. In 1920, for the first time, the census found the majority of Americans living in urban areas, many recently displaced from their rural roots. The typical Klan recruit, a married man with children, would have been witness to dramatic and often threatening social and tech-nological changes taking place around him. Challenges to the old way of life seemed everywhere: radio, telephone, airplanes, affordable automobiles, movies, and a more open attitude about sexuality. Women now had the vote, and violation of Prohibition was widely flaunted. The economic crash of 1920 raised the specter of job competition from blacks and foreign immigrants who were willing to work for less. The Klan spoke

---

[4] By order of the Imperial Wizard, Klan membership was secret, hence such numbers are extrapolated by historians from fragmentary data. Some estimates put the Klan's maximum membership as high as five million-plus in the 1923–1925 time frame.

for the common man, the "one hundred percent American." Moreover, the Klan promised action, not mere words.

For all its professed morality, the Klan had a dark side. While each chapter recognized the central tenants of "Americanism," local actions varied widely. In Wrightsville and Johnson County, the Klan took root easily. In Sandersville and Washington County, only nineteen miles to the north, the influence of the Klan was less prominent. Despite the Klan's avowed anti-Semiticism and anti-Catholic stances, neither group was consistently harassed. Both cities, like many southern towns, had well-assimilated Jewish merchants, and those who professed the Roman Catholic faith were rare. The blacks, necessary to the economy and suppressed through years of institutional racism, were harassed only if they violated some perceived moral or social code. In Georgia, the "Klan seldom directed its violence toward Jew, Roman Catholic and Negro. They were objects of its semantics, but its direct action was visited primarily on its fellow white, native-born Protestants."[5]

Some displays of morality were public. The *Sandersville Progress* reported on the Klan's holding a midnight "prohibition jubilee" as "several thousand Klansmen" in full regalia led a parade around a burning moonshine still as Prohibition officially came into effect on January 17, 1920. Other actions were taken behind the anonymity of the hooded mask. Later that year, the *Progress* reprinted an "official decree" from Imperial Wizard Simmons publicly condemning "night riders" dressed in Klan regalia who had been threatening cotton gin owners and burning gins in an effort to lower cotton production to stifle supply and raise prices.

The largest public threat of the Klan, however, arose from its self-anointed role as moral enforcer. Individuals who came

[5] Chalmers 1987, 71.

to the Klan's attention because of failure to conform to the group's version of morality were often physically punished. Most often, those adjudged guilty by the Klan were accused of sins not regulated by law—infidelity, failure to support one's family, wife beating, drunkenness, and the like. Requests for intervention came from aggrieved wives or concerned neighbors, or were sifted from small-town gossip. When appropriate, an investigation would be made, and if the charges were substantiated, the offender would be warned, often with an anonymous note and at times with a visit from masked men.

For those who chose to ignore the Klan's warnings, the consequences could be severe. Although many—perhaps most—such interventions went unreported, newspaper reports and court records from Georgia and across the nation documented floggings, beatings, tar-and-featherings, and sometimes murder of those targeted for punishment.[6] Law enforcement officials, many of whom may have been Klan members themselves, often turned a blind eye. The public at large was not displeased to see at least some action taken against a perceived decline in morals. This failure to enforce the rule of law seemed to "lay not so much in the willingness of Klansmen to regulate society as it lay in the willingness of the larger group to let them regulate."[7]

As the Klan's numbers and political strength grew, many politicians embraced the organization either by joining or by offering support. Thomas E. Watson, the powerful populist demagogue, endorsed its goals.[8] Others, rightfully fearing its nighttime raids and extra-legal activities, sought to weaken it. One of the reasons for the Klan's failure to have more influence

---

[6] Hux 1978; MacLean 1994, 149ff.

[7] Jackson 1967, 68.

[8] Woodward 1963, 449.

in Washington County was the opposition of Tom Hardwick, one of Georgia's senators from 1914 through 1919, and victor in the state gubernatorial election of 1920. Standing with him was Ben Rawlings, Charlie's brother and the governor's former law partner. Ben had served in the state legislature and had expressed vigorous opposition to both Watson and the Klan. As governor, Hardwick proposed an anti-mask law directed at the Klan. When he ran for reelection in 1922, he lost to the Klan-backed candidate, Clifford Walker, in "one of the biggest electoral defeats in state history."[9]

The exact timing and details of what happened to Charlie Rawlings will never be known. It is unlikely that his brother's opposition to the Klan played a role in its decision to punish him; Charlie was perfectly capable of arousing the Klan's wrath on his own. He had, over the years, sired several mixed-race children with local black women. He had money and, in the words of one informant, "was bad to run around," having a number of girlfriends and mistresses. Another tale had him involved with an underage girl. Whatever his sin, he was rich, he was arrogant, and he had been warned by the Klan. He was being watched, and someone knew his schedule.

The trap was laid on a rural dirt road in Johnson County. The Klan knew he would drive that way; his chauffeur-driven Cadillac was easily identified. Rounding a curve, his black driver, Hal Hooks, found his way blocked by a large limb that appeared to have fallen in the road. When he stopped to remove it, armed and masked men immediately surrounded the car. They jerked Charlie from the car and warned his driver not to move. There, under the glare of his headlights, they castrated him. The job was said to be expertly done, possibly indicating that the wielder of the knife was a professional or at

[9] MacLean 1994, 18.

156

least had experience in those matters. The cutting finished, they threw him back into his car with the suggestion that his physician-brother, also a Klan opponent, sew him up. Hooks drove him to Sandersville, where his brother stopped the bleeding and saved his life.

The incident, which likely occurred in 1921, was never reported to the authorities. Perhaps the scissors in the coal had indeed been an omen.[10]

---

[10] For additional information on the Ku Klux Klan and recommended reading, please see the "Chapter Notes" section near the end of the book.

19

Justice Dispensed

With his world and life's achievements falling apart, his wife dead, and his brothers suing him, Charlie Rawlings withdrew from public view. Now that he was under indictment for arson, his continued service as president of the Citizens Bank would appear unseemly, to say the least. He resigned, handing the office and salary to his son-in-law, W. A. Wray. This endowment would eventually prove to be as worthy as the gift of the oil mill, but Wray gamely accepted the position and tried to make the best of it. While Charlie remained the bank's major stockholder, his name was severed from its operations.

Charlie did retain his position as president of the Sandersville Railroad, but, like other businesses across the cotton belt, short-line railroads were also facing devastating losses. In December 1921, Charles Molony, president and general manager of the Wadley Southern Railway Company and the Louisville and Wadley Railroad Company,[1] took out a full-page ad in the *Sandersville Progress* to respond to various complaints and criticisms of the lines' services that had appeared in local newspapers. Both lines joined the main Central of Georgia route in Tennille, hauling freight and passengers back and forth from neighboring Jefferson County.

---

[1] By 1930, Molony would be president of four short-line railroads.

Confronting his detractors with the "plain blunt facts," Molony made it abundantly clear that both railroads had been losing money at an ever-increasing rate. Racked between decreasing gross revenues and inflation-driven cost increases, he asserted that the owners would be fully justified in abandoning the roads and discontinuing operations. His were not the only small rail lines facing bankruptcy. "During the past few months," he reported, "the Georgia Coast & Piedmont, a 100 mile road; the Valdosta, Moultrie & Western, a 40 mile road, and the Florida Southern, a 95 mile road, have all ceased operation. The Tennessee, Alabama & Georgia, a 90 mile road, is about to be junked and many other Short Lines are headed for oblivion. I cannot tell what the future of [the] Short Lines will be...." He might have added the Sandersville Railroad to his list. While still financially viable, its future was equally uncertain, and Charlie Rawlings knew that.

Additionally, the final ginning report for 1921 confirmed the earlier predictions and fears of a short cotton crop. Washington County had produced only 4,492 bales of cotton, about a third of the 1920 crop, and a sixth of the usual production in the glory days before the weevil's arrival.

The economic unease was reflected in a deep sense that society was headed in the wrong direction. Riding on this wave was the Ku Klux Klan with its calls for a restoration of old-time morality and its attempts to blame the nation's woes on Jews, blacks, and Catholics. Perhaps inspired by the Klan, or perhaps with Klan members among them, a mob of "determined white men" armed with rifles and tracking dogs pursued a black man accused of "an unmentionable crime" from Johnson County into Washington County, eager to administer vigilante justice.

As the Klan gained members and notoriety, a letter signed by "An Old Citizen," purportedly a Civil War veteran, was featured prominently on the front page of the local paper. The writer condemned the secret order, noting that "between our white and colored citizens harmony prevails." But in his call for the rule of law, the writer failed to recognize the fundamental plight of the average black farm laborer or share-cropper, stating, "You know as well as I do the best labor for us to work are negroes. They understand us and we understand them." What he seemed incapable of understanding himself was that the old system was dying, something no amount of rhetoric could change. The northward and urban migration of African Americans, temporarily stymied by the brief Great Recession, would resume with a vengeance in mid- to late 1922.

The long-anticipated trial of Charlie Rawlings for the charge of arson began on Thursday afternoon, March 9. With his usual lawyer now serving as governor, Charlie had hired a gaggle of local and regional attorneys to represent him. Judge Robert N. Hardeman, a severe-countenanced Prohibitionist who favored bowties and horn-rimmed glasses, presided. The prosecution opened with the state fire marshall giving evidence that the oil mill fire appeared to have been deliberately set. When H. T. Brown, the night watchman who had given a full signed confession, was placed on the stand, "his memory failed." He was unable to remember anything of either the fire or his previous sworn statement. As was usual with such high-profile cases, a large crowd was present. Following Brown's testimony, "it was openly stated by the spectators that the state had failed to make out their case."

ROBERT N. HARDEMAN

Judge Robert N. Hardeman, an ardent prohibitionist, presided over the arson trial of Charlie Rawlings.

The following day, the defense presented several witnesses, after which Judge Hardeman charged the jury and sent them off for their deliberations. With a signed confession—in spite of the witness's loss of memory—the case against Rawlings seemed certain. Three jurors, however, were not entirely clear on the law and asked the judge for clarification. Soon thereafter, they returned a verdict of not guilty, acquitting Charlie of all charges against him. Justice had been served. Or, more likely, purchased.

The trial of H. T. Brown, the confessed co-conspirator, was set for the following Monday. He entered a plea of insanity, which was quickly confirmed by a jury, sending him quietly to the state asylum in Milledgeville until his mental health improved. The trials of the "several negroes" indicted with Rawlings and Brown were "deferred indefinitely."

As spring wore on, the business community continued to suffer. In Bartow, the once-thriving hamlet and center of cotton production in southern Jefferson County, the stock of three of the leading local merchants was being sold at a bankruptcy sale. Cotton prices had nearly doubled in fall 1921 as compared to their low point earlier in the year, and were hovering in the fifteen- to sixteen-cent range in winter 1922. While the price would have been a good one a few years earlier, the effect of the 1916–1920 inflation had so devalued the dollar's buying power that even that price did not ensure a profit, resulting in the failure of merchants whose income was closely linked to farm income. By June, however, a number of farmers who had been holding out for higher prices sold their cotton in the twenty-cent range, once more inflating hopes of a return to the easy profit days not long past.

In the dark days of 1921 when cotton's price was scraping bottom, many farmers had sworn to diversify their crops and wean themselves from the white fiber's addiction. But, like sinners after a revival-driven come-to-Jesus moment, they were rapidly backsliding into their old ways. In June, the editor of the *Progress* observed that the "lure of cotton is still strong," and farmers were planting more for the 1922 crop year. The obvious reason was simple: "This is the one production of the farm which can be converted into cash at any hour of the day or any day of the year, and for this reason it has always been regarded as the south's money crop. The recent rapid rise in the price has had the effect of stimulating interest in the production of this crop, as every farmer wants to make all that he can."

As the crop season progressed, however, the outlook once again dimmed. By mid-August, the consensus—based on an informal survey of farmers who had come to town on a Saturday morning—predicted a crop "about the same" size as that of the previous year, itself a record disaster due to the boll weevil. The farmers who had invested in machinery and calcium arsenate found their hopes "dashed to pieces by the swarms of weevils that have survived the applications." Prices were "expected to advance sharply" when the preliminary crop reports came out, but this would be of little comfort to those farmers who had nothing to sell. By year's end, the county had produced somewhat in excess of 5,000 bales, not a great improvement over 1921.

As landowners diversified and sought other sources of income, there was increasing interest in the extensive clay deposits lying along the geologic fall line from Augusta to the area southwest of Macon. The railroads, especially the Central of Georgia, took the lead in promoting this natural resource, recognizing that rail cars full of clay would pay just as well as rail cars filled with cotton. Extensive clay beds had been exposed in digging railroad rights of way. The ill-fated oil well project, if nothing else, confirmed that these beds were not only near the surface and easily accessible but also of great depth and quantity.

In early spring, 1922, the railroad sent its geologist to survey the prospects of a large commercial mining industry for bauxite, kaolin, and other clays, announcing that "they would not hesitate to place train tracks to connect the mines with the main line, for the freight would be a financial inducement." By May, the decision had been made. Plans were underway to build a five-mile spur to ship out "as fine deposits as can be found in the United States." Resources were said to be "sufficient to supply the needs of this nation for generations to come," with "glowing opportunities" for future development. The good news could not have failed to be music to the ears of large, local landowners—provided, of course, that they were able to hold on to their property long enough to see the industry develop.

Social unrest continued. A mid-year report from Booker T. Washington's Tuskegee Institute found that in the first six months of the year, only thirty lynchings had taken place across the south, down six from the same period in 1921, but eighteen more than the relatively prosperous first half of 1920. Twenty-eight of the thirty victims were black, with rape being the most common single crime of which they were accused.

In late September, the local area contributed another statistic. Jim Johnson, a negro from Wrightsville, was being held in the Washington County jail for "safe keeping" because of local threats of lynching. Early on a Thursday morning, the local sheriff was awakened by two deputies and a third man from Johnson County who appeared at the jail to pick up the prisoner and carry him back to Wrightsville for trial. The odd hour for transport was designed "to avoid any possible trouble." Just outside of Wrightsville, an organized and well-armed "posse of fifty citizens" ambushed the deputies and hauled away the prisoner. He was taken to Cedar Creek Bridge, three miles from town, "where he was strung up to a tree and riddled with bullets." More than two hundred shots were fired into his body.

The local paper reported that "the negro confessed just before he was strung up," but there was more to the story. Local lore states that when asked if he had any last words, Johnson cursed the legal system and decreed that the Johnson County courthouse clock "would never tell good time." More than a decade and a half later, his curse would allegedly lead to a strange event involving the clock.

20

"Laborers Drift to the North"[1]

A s rural Georgia's economic crisis entered its fourth year, subtle signs indicated that if things were not improving, at least they might be stabilizing. The boll weevil was every bit the menace predictions had held it to be, but now there was increasing evidence that through careful selection of seeds and soil, plus the conscientious applications of arsenates, reasonable and predictable cotton yields could be expected. With the start of the 1923 crop season, the papers were full of ads for products like Hill's Mixture ("The Boll Weevil Exterminator"), Weevilnip ("Highly Endorsed by Some of the Largest and Leading Planters"), and Wee-VO ("Guaranteed to Kill the Boll Weevil or Money Refunded"). Cotton prices, which had climbed above twenty cents a pound in mid-1922, gradually rose, reaching the twenty-five-cent mark early in the new year.

There was a smattering of new businesses. In Midville, W. A. Wray and two other businessmen were in the process of opening a large lumber-planing mill on the site of one of Charlie Rawlings's fertilizer plants, now defunct due to lack of demand. The Bank of Harrison, which had eventually failed after the suicide of J. H. Arnold, had been bought by Lake B. Holt and was to be reopened as a private bank, later to become part of the Holt Banking Company chain. It was the only local banking casualty of the economy thus far, and, operating as a private institution, it would not be subject to requirements that

---

[1] Headline from the *Sandersville Progress*, 10 January 1923.

it publicly reveal its financial condition. The county's ten other banks were said to be in good shape, but only two of them would survive the decade.

Once again, the annual news story announcing the fine condition of the Citizens Bank was conspicuous by its absence. Meanwhile, the First National Bank, Lake Holt's flagship business, trumpeted its twenty-first consecutive annual 12 percent dividend. The bank deemed itself "one of the best managed financial institutions of the state..., especially at this time when so many banks are liquidating on account of unprofitable business."

While some read recovery and growth in the crystal ball of the future, others were forced by circumstances and finances to seek their fortunes elsewhere. For blacks, the specter of the Ku Klux Klan and the threat of mob justice carried out by lynching was reason enough. But for farmers of all races seeking to provide a decent living and future for themselves and their families, there was a more fundamental reason: farming had ceased to be profitable. It was estimated that for the average Georgia farm, cash income in 1922–1923 was $271 per year, a bit more than $5 per week. To make matters worse, the buying power of the dollar had fallen dramatically with inflation during the last years of the Wilson administration. The Great Recession was officially over, and while small-town Georgia suffered, the rest of the nation was undergoing a period of rapid economic growth.

The so-called Great Migration, a term that generally refers to the exodus of African Americans from the South, spanned roughly the period between 1910 and the start of World War II. Most significant for the state of Georgia was the loss of black citizens in the early to mid-1920s following the Great Recession of 1920–1921 and the accompanying collapse of cotton as a profitable crop. While the focus of historians has often been on black emigration, the exodus also extended to white tenant farmers who faced the same dire economic outlook, if not the additional problem of state-sanctioned racism. Like other significant periods of internal migration, for example the exodus from the mid-west Dust Bowl of the 1930s, the outcome of this period of departure of the small landless farmer was one of profound demographic, political, and social change in both the North and the South.

In the Georgia of the early 1920s, the majority of farms was operated by tenants whose net income reflected that of the farms. Moreover, there was a striking disparity between the status of white and black farmers. According to the 1920 United States Census, nearly 52 percent of white farmers were tenants, most of whom would have operated their land on a sharecropping basis. For blacks, however, 87.5 percent, or some seven out of eight farmers, were listed as tenants. With no ownership of the land, few obligations beyond local debt and family connections, and a plunge in income, it was only natural for them to seek better fortunes in other locations. Beginning with the arrival of the boll weevil, followed by the collapse of cotton prices in 1920, and worsened by the subsequent failure of banks, merchants, and other businesses, the reasons for staying were often outweighed by the chance of a better life elsewhere.

Many, perhaps most, black emigrants moved north to cities such as Detroit and Philadelphia. While some southern whites may have also sought economic security in the North, many moved to the larger cities of the state, resulting in a period of record growth for Georgia's urban areas. By the first quarter of the century, many of the textile mills that had so characterized the northeastern states in the nineteenth century were well established in the South. Hence, mill towns like Columbus and Rome experienced periods of intense growth, while nearby cotton-producing counties lost population.

For Georgia, the tipping point in terms of loss of farm labor seemed to arrive in late 1922 and early 1923. The post-recession recovery of the northern industrial economy, laws restricting European immigration, and the continued depression of the farm economy made the rural South a fertile hunting ground for labor agents, paid on commission to attract workers for employment in the North. The *Sandersville Progress* began 1923 with a front-page article expressing local concerns that "farms will be left without enough help" for the upcoming crop season. Some farmers, worried about the labor scarcity, planned to cut back on their planted acreage. "People from various sections of the county," the paper noted, "report that there has been an exodus of some of the most desirable laborers, and the farmers are now facing a labor shortage which will mean a curtailment of all kinds of crops."

Rather than recognizing that the emigration of laborers, sharecroppers, and others was a social and economic phenomenon, local and statewide attitudes seemed to place much of the blame on elusive labor agents, whose work was "done on sly, and then they skip." The *Progress* pointed out, "There is a law governing labor agents, which is not generally known by the people. They have no right to entice the laborers away unless they have complied with the law; but their operations are secret and the people who are affected by their acts are not aware of what is happening until it is too late to interfere."

In early February, H. M. Stanley, head of the state Department of Commerce and Labor, issued a letter to all sheriffs and chiefs of police in the state. He warned,

> The emigrant agents are carrying negroes out of the state by the hundreds every day, and unless something is done to stop this exodus of labor the farmers and manufacturers will soon be without labor…. Now this department does not have a force large enough to cover the whole state and unless the sheriffs and policemen in each county and city get busy and see to it that there be no recruiting of labor to be transported from their respective counties out of the state, Georgia will soon be depleted of its common laborers. Each county and locality will have to look after this matter locally as this department has not the funds or the men to cover the state.

He closed with the admonition to "do your part to protect the interest of the people against these labor agents." It was an invitation to apply locally interpreted justice with little regard for the rights of either the laborers or the agents.

By mid-May, hard into the most critical time for crops, a number of farmers in Washington County reported being "badly handicapped…on account of the scarcity of labor" as "the tide of this movement to the north continues unabated."[2] In the first five months of the year, the Georgia State College of Agriculture estimated that 100,000 people, more than 80 percent of them African Americans, had left the farms of the state to seek employment elsewhere. In these same five months, it was estimated that nearly 12,000 farms had been abandoned.

Harking back to the emigration-induced labor shortage of the war years, the local papers were once again full of stories of the dire consequences that awaited blacks who were foolish enough to venture north: "Disease resulting from living conditions in the North are taking a heavy toll of [sic] negroes who have been enticed away from Georgia by labor agents with

---

[2] *Sandersville Progress*, 16 May 1923.

extravagant promises of high wages." This was reported to have been verified by "heads of negro insurance companies" who found that "the percentages of deaths among their policy holders who have moved north is far higher than among those who have remained in the south." Ben Davis, said to be "the editor of an Atlanta newspaper for negroes," "urged the educated negroes to show the members of their race the folly of blindly accepting the statement of labor agents who are paid so much a head for the negroes they can sign up."

The frustration of farmers even expressed itself in resentment of the railroads that carried the laborers north. An exchange of correspondence between B. E. Thrasher, a planter from Plains, Georgia, and W. A. Winburn, president of the Central of Georgia Railway Company, was typical. Thrasher contended that the railroad could, if it chose, "apprehend every labor agent operating," essentially accusing the line of being more interested in money than justice. Winburn replied that as common carriers, rail lines could neither "refuse business" nor make arrests "on suspicion of illegal activity." He in turn blamed "immigration laws designed to create a shortage of labor," thus allowing the emerging labor union movement of the North to demand wage increases. His suggestion was a revision of national immigration policy to exclude "the horde of undesirables," while "attracting to our shores that element from the northern countries of Europe which is most desirable." The ultimate solution, Winburn advised, was "dealing with certain local conditions which we in the South must do for ourselves." His statement reflected a glimmer of reason in an otherwise confused world.

By summer it was clearly recognized that the growing collapse of Georgia's farm economy was neither something transient nor another cyclical downturn to be weathered until times improved. The infrastructure that had for so many decades supported small-town life was crumbling, with businesses, banks, and farmers alike seeing little light at the end of the tunnel. In response, the Macon Chamber of Commerce, in cooperation with area communities, launched the Middle Georgia Development Program. Then-current estimates by the Georgia College of Agriculture found that within a sixty-mile radius of Macon, there were some 4,000,000 acres of idle land, of which 3,000,000 were available for cultivation.[3] The goal of the program was "to promote the intensive cultivation of all farm lands in Middle Georgia."

From Abbeville to Eatonton, committees were organized in each city and county to take photographs of "good crops, livestock, farm homes or barns, or other pictures showing the advantages" of the particular area. These were to become part of a nationwide publicity program aimed especially at "farmers from the North and Middle West." There were plans to emulate a similar effort in Greenwood County, South Carolina, to offer "free farm lands to thrifty and intelligent white farmers, to take the place of negroes who have migrated to the north." Ten thousand copies of a special edition of *Macon Magazine* were to be published and distributed in areas from which immigrant farmers could be recruited.

Despite all, the exodus of laborers and tenant farmers continued. Even as local chambers of commerce sought to attract farmers to the area, other distant states were seeking to attract Georgia's farmers to *their* lands. In August, just as the outlook for the cotton crop dimmed once again, an ad by the Halsell

---

[3]The figures for idle land are astounding. To put them in perspective by comparison, the total land area of Bibb County (Macon being the largest city) is approximately 160,000 acres, and for Washington County 435,520 acres.

Farms Company of Lamb County, Texas, touted, "No Boll
Weevil! Big Crops—Cheap Land." Aimed at tenant farmers,
here was an opportunity to "make some real money—and to
own this new land on easy terms—less than rent in most
places."[4]

Cotton prices stayed high and increased for most of the
year, ending the harvest season above thirty cents a pound.
The state government had done what it could, buying a million
pounds of calcium arsenate and in turn reselling it at cost in
railcar lots to farmers, hoping to suppress the weevil infestation. By June, however, weevils were once again numerous,
with one Washington County farmer reporting "he [had] never
seen as many boll weevils at this season of the year as are now
to be found on the young cotton stalks." Even with pesticides
available, most farmers could not afford mechanized equipment to apply them, and the shortage of labor made hand
application impractical. Near the end of the harvest season in
mid-November, it was estimated that the state's cotton crop
would be the lowest since 1878, due to a combination of
decreased planting and destruction by the weevil. The final
crop report for the year showed that Washington County had
produced somewhat in excess of a thousand bales over 1922,
but it was still in the range of a quarter of a former good year's
yield.

Charlie Rawlings continued to maintain a low profile for
most of the year. His son-in-law, W. A. Wray, had become the
face of the Citizens Bank, running regular upbeat ads that
extolled the bank's safety and security, while throwing himself
into the process of making money in difficult times. He was
now a well-known man about town, with dark, sharply parted
hair and a penchant for bowties. Setting his sights beyond

---

[4] *Sandersville Progress*, 15 August 1923.

Sandersville, he embraced the new technology and became known as a "radio-bug" who had the instruments and skill to listen to transmitters from as far away as Havana, Cuba. Speaking to the local Kiwanis Club, he urged Sandersville to adopt the attitude of Atlanta, to "bend every effort to secure anything that was good" for the community. And he appeared to be successful. His planer mill in Midville, now known as the Wray-Joiner Company of which he was president, "was running day and night to keep up with [the] constantly increasing orders for dressed lumber." He lived in Sandersville but was tapping into the boom that was sweeping the rest of the nation.

Others were doing well also, in some part due to Charlie Rawlings's withdrawal from business life. Lewis Holt (a relative of Lake) had become the predominant local dealer in mules, having sold "thousands" over the years, as well as buggies and wagons. He had expanded into shipping in coal from Kentucky and developed a thriving business in farm supplies. Lake Holt himself had also set his sights on riches beyond the county line, purchasing the Balmere Apartments in downtown Atlanta, "considered one of the most valuable pieces of property in the capital city." The transaction was handled by the Holt Realty Company of Atlanta.

Still others, perhaps wiser, saw a different future. Louis Cohen, once the county's richest man and still near the top in terms of wealth, announced in December 1923 that he was closing his bank after thirty-eight years in business, citing that "this was an opportune time." The bank was "the first established between Macon and Savannah, and [was] one of Georgia's oldest and best known banking institutions."

Desperate for cash, many landowners were turning to harvesting timber to make ends meet. It was estimated that nearly five hundred sawmills were operating within a twenty-five-mile radius of Sandersville, with "lumber being hauled into [the city] day and night." Late in the year, Charlie Rawlings pulled together a major deal to sell timber from his estimated 30,000 acres in Johnson and Washington counties. The $100,000 cash he received represented the largest such transaction ever recorded in the area and earned front-page headlines in the local paper. When asked about "the cotton situation," he expressed faith that the post-weevil price increases were enough to make him want to continue growing the fiber.

In Johnson County, Gus Tarbutton must have been suffering. He was one of the largest cotton farmers in the county and, like others, was reeling from the effects of the weevil. At the end of 1922, he owned some 7,750 acres of land, the vast majority of which was under cultivation. As of the end of 1923, however, he owned nothing. A new entity had appeared on the tax records, the firm of Rawlings & Tarbutton, owned equally by C. G. Rawlings and Gus Tarbutton. The partnership owned 2,040 acres, while the remainder of Gus's land, some 6,000 acres, was now in the name of Charlie Rawlings. A year later, the name of Rawlings & Tarbutton had disappeared from the records, with Charlie Rawlings now personally owning the entire 8,040 acres.

From later court testimony, it appears that these transactions took place because of the failure of the cotton crops in the early 1920s. Gus owed the Citizens Bank significant sums of money that he was unable to repay on schedule. Charlie had started Gus out in business, and perhaps he did not want to see his first cousin's life work lost in the embarrassment of a public bankruptcy. It would have been a simple matter to have Charlie assume the bank debt as well as the title to the land.

After all, for practical purposes Charlie owned the bank, and the land would have been held as collateral. As far as anyone needed to know, Gus could continue farming as before, hoping to regain title to his property once conditions—and profits—improved.

Assuming ownership of Gus's land was a gamble to be sure, a bet that cotton would return to its historic level of profitability. Charlie had taken gambles before and won. But he may have had other, less altruistic motives for assuming legal ownership of the land. It lay on the Oconee River, abutting Wilkinson County where extensive deposits of kaolin and bauxite had been found and were already being mined. It was just downriver from the village of Oconee, where the clay was said to be of "very superior quality." For months, there had been regular news stories of how the clay industry could bring "fortunes" to the local area. Here, perhaps with a bit of luck, was a solution to Charlie's financial troubles.

21

One Last Fire

The Citizens Bank had managed to survive 1923, but barely. The balance sheet looked dismal. While total deposits were up somewhat, they were still a fraction of what they were during the heady days of prosperity only a few years earlier. More important, the total amount of outstanding loans to borrowers had increased, and it still represented nearly three times the sum of all deposits. The concept of bank regulation was still in its infancy, and thus the institution continued with business as usual.

The bank's ads under W. A. Wray had taken on a chatty nature, dispensing the kind of sage advice that a father might impart to a son just entering the world of business. One such ad in February 1924 could have been directed at Charlie Rawlings. It read, in part, "Ahead of you is old age, waiting. There is the old age, dignified, independent, happy—the best time in life when foolish fires have died out, regretted follies almost forgotten, no more harm or falsehood need be feared, and the mind, mature, studies life and other worlds quietly and hopefully. [Then] there is the old age toward which so many are drifting—the old age of poverty, sorrow, humiliation and dependence." The text went on to urge saving while one was young, but for Charlie it was too late. He was sixty-five now, widowed, alone, and trying to hold his world together in a time of rapid change. He had already suffered sorrow and humiliation, and now he faced the prospect of poverty and dependence.

The world at large seemed to be coming apart. In Atlanta, the new young wife of the elderly Coca-Cola magnate Asa G. Candler was arrested while drinking whiskey in an apartment with two men. Her excuse was, "We are having a little party. I don't see any harm in that." The decline in morality had spread to local high school athletic meets. The *Washington* (GA) *News-Reporter* opined, "With the gaiety and hilarity which attend these football and baseball and field events in schools, at which whiskey drinking and all-night orgies are common, in which girls participate as well as the boys, these school meets are becoming menaces to the future of the race and it is time that the parents of the young folks were awakening to the seriousness of the situation, if the school facilities are blind to them."[1] Even the Klan had made inroads into Washington County, organizing a chapter in Tennille and holding barbecues and other public functions.

Bank and business failures continued. George Brinson, a "noted railroad builder" of three lines in southeast Georgia, declared bankruptcy in June. In Hancock County, where cotton production had created vast wealth in the late nineteenth and early twentieth centuries, the economy claimed its fourth bank failure of the decade. Charles E. Choate, a decade earlier the widely sought architect of the homes of the rich and famous, was forced to shutter his firm and move to Florida where he found a bureaucratic job with the State Hotel Commission.[2] Even Charlie's bother, the respected Dr. William Rawlings, was being sued by the Georgia Cotton Growers Association for failure to deliver some 324 bales of cotton promised in 1923 as

---

[1] The article from the *News-Reporter* was quoted in the *Sandersville Progress* of May 14, 1924, "as a warning to parents who want to raise their children in ways that are right."

[2] Rawlings 2009.

part of a cooperative sales contract. Despite being "one of the largest landowners in Washington County," as well as the proprietor of a busy hospital and successful dairy and purebred cattle operation, he was unable to meet his contractual obligations.

For those who managed to avoid overt failure, the times called for more modest expectations. The Masons, having given up on the magnificent three-story replacement for their meeting hall that had been destroyed more than three years earlier, settled on a far less pretentious two-story building. Despite the nominal wealth of its members, they were unable to find financing and resorted to issuing private bonds in small denominations to be repaid over the coming decade.

As spring wore on and farmers began their planting season, a small notice advertising "Bank Stock For Sale" appeared at the bottom of the front page of the Sandersville paper. It advertised twenty shares of capital stock in the Citizens Bank, which were available "at a great bargain or [in] exchange for liberty bonds or any other stock listed on the exchange." Even though the bank publicly posted its required balance sheet statements, perhaps only an insider among the bank's few shareholders might have recognized its desperate financial plight. Thereafter the bank's advertising abruptly ceased, and, while it was still open for business, little more would be heard of it publicly until the fateful spring of the following year.

In mid-June, the first cotton blossom of the year was reported from one of Charlie Rawlings's farms in Washington County. With the addition of Gus Tarbutton's land, his holdings were now near 40,000 acres, much of it under cultivation. He was said to be "very optimistic over the prospects for a fine crop for 1924." Perhaps he had been encouraged by the increasing price of cotton for the 1923–1924 season, with a peak of 32.5 cents a pound in January 1924. Little could he or anyone else have known that prices were about to begin a long decline that would persist for decades. If the second Golden Age of Cotton needed a final nail in its coffin, it was now being struck.

The same issue of the paper also carried the headline, "Fire Destroys Large Stable." Charlie Rawlings's livery stable had burned to the ground, a complete loss. Like its owner, it had become a shadow of its former self "since the demand for farm and timber stock became slack on account of the depression in agricultural conditions and the use of trucks in hauling lumber." The space had been divided and some of it rented out, part to a garage, part to a pressing club,[3] and part for the stabling of animals. Several vehicles were burned, including two of Charlie's and one of W. A. Wray's (his son-in-law). Two mules and several hogs died, with the other tenants suffering significant losses also. There was not "a cent of insurance" on the building or any of its contents.

Personal tragedy was not limited to Sandersville. On August 4, Gus Tarbutton's forty-four-year-old wife, Donnie, succumbed to a bout of typhoid. She had been sick for about ten days and died quietly at the Tarbuttons' "beautiful country home." The funeral was in Sandersville at the home of Ben Tarbutton, after which Donnie was laid to rest in the family plot next to the grave of her brother-in-law, Herschel, who had been killed in the shootout with Lecher Tyre in 1906.

---

[3] A "pressing club" was a cooperative in which members paid a monthly fee to have certain nicer garments maintained. This generally included cleaning, spot removal, minor repairs, and, of course, pressing.

Though Charlie Rawlings's fortune began with his livery stable, by the early 1920s mechanized equipment was beginning to replace equine power. The stable was destroyed by fire in 1924.

The northward migration of African Americans continued unabated. Threats, scare tactics, and attempts at reasoning all seemed to have failed, so the local paper turned to the most obvious tactic—the announcement that there was no more work in the North. Citing a resolution by the city council of East St. Louis, Missouri, the *Progress* announced "that there are no jobs awaiting the colored people of the south who decide to go north, as all demands for their services have been filled." It is highly improbable that many of the would-be emigrants paid the story much mind.

Some local citizens kept up an air of optimism, often flying in the face of reality. W. A. Wray entertained the Kiwanis Club in late July with the "very optimistic" prediction that the county would produce 20,000 bales of cotton for the year, more than three times the crop for the 1923 season.[4] Ever the public citizen, he urged support for an effort to pave the muddy City Square, even offering to join in loaning money to the city for the project, though his balance sheet indicated he had no funds to loan.

Another guest at the same meeting brought up a more practical idea, however. A man from Gordon, a small town in adjacent Wilkinson County, spoke of the need for a bridge over the Oconee between the two counties. Wilkinson was becoming a hub of industrial activity with a new paper mill and kaolin mines generating a payroll of more than a million dollars annually.

As the year drew to a close, economic prospects for the nascent mining industry assumed greater importance. The Georgia White Brick Company announced plans to build a large brick plant near Gordon, only twenty miles from Tennille. A week later it was announced that the Kalbfleisch

---

[4] The final figure was approximately half this amount.

Corporation[5] of New York had optioned 2,000 acres of land in Wilkinson County, seven miles south of the village of Toomsboro and only a few miles west of the former property of Gus Tarbutton, now owned by Charlie Rawlings. Bauxite deposits, said to compare favorably with other known deposits in Arkansas and elsewhere, had been discovered. Mining operations were to start early in 1925.

One other small item in the weekly paper probably passed unnoticed by the majority of Sandersville's citizens in late 1924. It was the announcement that the state, having decided to electrocute condemned men instead of hanging them, had elected to locate the new electric chair in the main building of the State Prison Farm in Milledgeville, thirty miles west of Sandersville. The site had the advantage of already having a 2,300-volt electric line in place, "a sufficient amount to produce instant insensibility and painless death." It was the sort of information most folks would assume they'd never be forced to consider.[6]

---

[5] Later to become part of American Cyanamid Corporation.

[6] The *Wrightsville Headlight* reported that the "death chair" was put to use on Saturday, September 14, 1924, after "the first victim had been brought as a try-out." He was Howard Hinton, a negro from Dekalb County convicted of "criminal assault." The brief account of his execution was gruesome: "This death chair was built by prisoners at the farm and is said not to have been altogether in perfect trim at the time although it did work after much preliminaries going on and the victim hearing it all and taking it all in. From the newspaper accounts given it must have been an awful ordeal beforehand. This, however, can be and will be eliminated and the chair worked all right." "Several prominent Georgians" were said to be present to see how the new device worked. Commenting editorially, the paper's writer noted, "Hanging is no more in Georgia except perchance it be an illegal one somewhere sometimes." Johnson County was known for its lynchings.

22

A Tragic Accident

Nineteen twenty-five, the year that would forever change the life of Charlie Rawlings, began with a positive note of sorts. A January 1 front-page headline in the *Atlanta Constitution* announced "Only 16 Negroes Lynched in 1924," a small milestone for the fact that the number was less than half that of the preceding year. The second most common alleged offense among this group, after "criminal assault,"[1] was listed as "insulting women," an indication that a certain perverted sense of chivalry was still alive and well across the South. Of the sixteen lynchings, only two were said to have taken place in Georgia.

The winds of change continued to sweep across the land. Southern legislators squabbled over the teaching of evolution in the schools in a dispute that would lead to the infamous *State of Tennessee v. John Thomas Scopes* "Monkey Trial" in Tennessee later in the year. In Georgia, the renowned sculptor (and Ku Klux Klan member) John Gutzon de la Mothe Borglum was engaged in a harsh dispute with the Stone Mountain Confederate Memorial Association over his work on the massive carving planned for the rock outcropping near Atlanta. The project was being jointly funded by the United Daughters of the Confederacy, the Ku Klux Klan, and the federal government via the sale of Stone Mountain Memorial

---

[1] "Criminal assault" was used in this context as a euphemism for the alleged crime of rape.

Half Dollars, available at local banks for twice their face value. Borglum would later smash his clay and plaster models, leaving to move on to other works, the most famous of which would be the carving of the Mount Rushmore National Memorial in South Dakota.

Nature seemed once again bent on unleashing her fury on the state. Torrential rains, the worst in recent memory, caused massive flooding throughout south Georgia, destroying roads, bridges, and railroad lines alike. A large sinkhole opened up in downtown Sandersville near the city ice plant. Even the busy thoroughfare to Tennille became impassable, prompting one adjacent landowner to build a makeshift bridge and start charging tolls to would-be travelers. In late January an eclipse of the sun signaled portentous events to come for those foolish enough to believe in signs. The local paper editorialized against "the Liquor Evil," noting that "Anybody, the ruffian, the thug, the negro, the chauffeur, the cook, the landlord, the millionaire, the boy, the girl, the wife, the husband can procure it with almost as much ease as getting a consignment of ginger ale from the corner grocery."[2]

Not all was bad news. The final ginning tally for 1924 counted just over 10,000 bales of cotton produced in Washington County, an increase of more than 50 percent over the disastrous 1923 crop. The paper also reported that three carloads of mules had arrived the preceding week, suggesting that farmers were once again planning for the upcoming crop season. Lake Holt's First National Bank again announced a 12 percent dividend, declaring itself the "front bank of financial institutions in this section." And Charlie Rawlings, ever the optimist, was beginning to investigate the possibility of buried mineral riches on his first cousin's former property in Johnson County.

---

[2] *Sandersville Progress*, 14 January 1925.

Tarbutton's land, now belonging to Charlie Rawlings, lay along the east bank of the Oconee River. It was for the most part gently rolling land, the exception being the area where it bordered the river. Here was a long bluff where the earth dropped steeply to the river swamp below, falling in total nearly 200 feet from the plateau above.[3] This Ring Jaw Bluff, as it was called, ran more than a mile and a half along the river's edge, slashed here and there by springs, streams, and deep gullies cut into the earth by centuries of erosion. The origin of the Ring Jaw name had been lost in history, the most common explanation being that it was a corruption of a local Indian name in the Creek dialect.

Ring Jaw Bluff offered an ideal place for geologic exploration. Composed mainly of limestone and cretaceous sedimentary deposits, it was immediately adjacent to the well-established beds of alluvial kaolin that were abundant across the river in Wilkinson County.[4] Associated with these kaolin deposits were variable amounts of bauxite, valuable for its use as aluminum ore. The lay of the land on Ring Jaw Bluff with its gullies and the natural sharp drop toward the river simplified the investigation of multiple geologic layers. Commercial bauxite, kaolin, and clay mining were richly rewarding landowners just a few miles away. There was good reason to believe that valuable deposits might be found on the east side of the river as well.

---

[3] Since the 1920s, the course of the river in this area seems to have shifted westward a few hundred yards, such that portions of the bluff do not directly front on the stream. Such shifts are not uncommon among rivers in the relatively flat lands below the geologic fall line.

[4] Smith 1929; Lang 1965.

It wasn't as if Charlie Rawlings and Gus Tarbutton were at odds, at least not publicly. Their business and financial relationships were closely entwined and had been for years. The firm of Rawlings & Tarbutton had farming, mercantile, and timber interests in Johnson County. While the title to Gus's property had nominally changed hands, he continued to farm it as before, together with his side businesses of sawmill operations, his gin, and his country store. While others may have been struggling through the ongoing crisis in the farm economy, on the surface all seemed well between the two cousins. Gus had been quite involved in the exploration for bauxite on Ring Jaw Bluff. He had arranged for test pits to be dug and, if anything, considered this another joint venture.

The winter rains had slowed somewhat, and by mid-February the weather had turned unseasonably warm. The predictions for Tuesday, February 17, were for an overcast day with scattered showers and temperatures in the mid-sixties. In Sandersville that morning, the mail brought Charlie Rawlings some excellent news. The rock samples he had submitted for analysis from test pits dug on Ring Jaw Bluff had been found to contain high quantities of bauxite ore, sufficient amount to warrant—or at least seriously consider—commercial mining operations. The rain having let up after the midday meal, he stuffed the report in his jacket, called for his driver, Hal Hooks, and set out for Gus Tarbutton's house to show him the results.

Charlie arrived at Gus's house about mid-afternoon. Gus's son Fluker was there, together with his wife and small child, but Gus was out at one of the sawmills.[5] Charlie was said to be

---

[5] By way of clarification, much of the timber cut in rural Georgia through the mid-twentieth century was not hauled to large commercial sawmills as it is today, but rather cut on site into rough-sawn lumber, then stacked in ricks and left to dry in the open air for

in an ebullient mood and shared the good news with Fluker. They set out to find Gus, who was working about two miles away on the farm. Gus seemed equally pleased about the report and said that he wanted to show Charlie the test pits he was having dug on Ring Jaw Bluff. They left Fluker to oversee the sawmill operation while Charlie, Gus, and Hal Hooks headed toward the river, Gus driving the Cadillac with Charlie in the front seat and Hal, the chauffeur, in the back.

By the time they arrived at the site, it was getting late in the day. J. J. Tanner, one of Rawlings's overseers, met them at the end of the road near the steep part of the bluff. "Jim," as he was known to his family and friends, was sixty-three and had been working for Charlie for about a year. He was a thin, wiry man with large ears, deep-sunk eyes, and a long narrow nose that perched atop a huge handlebar moustache. He was carrying a hammerless double-barreled shotgun, something not unusual for a walk in the river swamp, even in mid-winter. Hooks stayed with the car while the other three set off in the direction of the river.

---

months, often as long as a year. House frames and sheeting would have been constructed from this lumber, but finished surfaces, such as floors, ceilings, and trim, would have been made from planed and milled stock, often the same air-dried lumber sent to a local millwork and/or planing mill. Through mid-century, "sawdust piles," sometimes quite large, dotted the rural landscape and were a frequent cause of accidental injury and death to children playing on them. The decaying sawdust interiors often reached high temperatures, causing burns, and at other times the piles would collapse and smother victims.

Jim Tanner was one of Charlie Rawlings's overseers and was accused of being the triggerman in the alleged plot to kill Gus Tarbutton. This photo was taken in the early 1920s.

The way down the slope was narrow, and the ground was slick from the day's rains, in addition to being laced with roots and vines. They walked single file, the younger Gus leading the way, then Jim, then Charlie. They stopped and inspected one test pit, a hole in the ground measuring about five feet by five feet, and equally as deep. Gus climbed down into the hole to have a look, then got out and proceeded ahead. As they neared the river the path became more treacherous. Charlie, feeling the effects of age and arthritis, lagged a bit behind the others. Jim, concerned about his employer's ability to negotiate the increasingly difficult terrain, turned to warn Charlie to be careful not to fall. Just as he did so, he himself slipped, in the process slamming the butt of the shotgun firmly into the earth. The shotgun fired. Gus teetered, then slumped forward, the back of his head blown off by the concentrated load of shot. Charlie, who had been looking ahead at the trail as he picked his way down the slope, glanced up at the sound of the gunshot just in time to see Jim sprawled on the ground and his cousin's lifeless body crumple to the earth.

Jim and Charlie rushed to where Gus had fallen. It was clear that there was nothing they could do. They began yelling for help, soon bringing Hal Hooks, rushing from the car, and Louis Stephens, another negro who had been working on a test pit further down the trail, to the scene. The time was between five and five-thirty in the afternoon. Darkness would descend shortly.

Together, the negroes and Tanner carried Gus's body back to the car, laying it in the back seat with Charlie. They drove to Gus's house, stopping in the yard under the now-barren winter oaks. Fluker and his wife were told of the tragedy, and the body was brought into the house to be prepared for burial. In the process, some of Gus's brain matter leaked from the gaping head wound and splattered on the ground. Charlie quickly directed one of the blacks to bury it, lest the dogs get into it. Soon friends, neighbors, and relatives began to gather at the house, all shocked by the sudden death of someone who was thought to be one of the most prosperous farmers in the area.

Fluker Tarbutton, twenty-two years old, was now the man of the house. Tragically thrust into this unexpected role by the death of his mother a scant six months earlier and now the sudden death of his father, he was angry. Angry at fate. Angry that his father, a man he had admired and depended on, had been snatched away. Angry with the man whom he thought caused it. Angry with Charlie Rawlings.

Charlie was devastated. It seemed that just when the future might look a shade brighter, misfortune struck once again. But he was a man of reason and a man of business. Among the many things that he may have said or done on the day that Gus Tarbutton died, one simple act was remembered. He asked about Gus's insurance.

In the hours that followed Gus's death, the initial feeling among the community at large was that there had been a tragic accident. Fluker Tarbutton believed otherwise. As the only son and heir, he assumed he had become the master of an 8,000-acre plantation, but he was soon to learn otherwise. How much he actually knew about his father's true financial condition or his relationship with Charlie Rawlings is impossible to tell. Fluker was aware that there were insurance policies, and he seemed to believe that he would be the beneficiary. He would later state that he and his father owned the land they farmed, not Charlie Rawlings. In Fluker's mind, his father had been murdered, and he set out to be certain that justice was served.

23

Was It Wanton Murder?

"Was Gus Tarbutton killed in cold blood by accident or was it wanton murder? This is the question that has been uppermost in minds of the people in three counties...." Thus read the opening lines of a front page, editorialized news report in the *Wrightsville Headlight* written the day after the killing. In eloquent prose, the writer subtly hinted that this tragedy was more than a simple mishap, noting that warrants had been issued for the arrests of those involved.

Gus Tarbutton's funeral was originally scheduled for Wednesday, February 18. He was to be buried in Sandersville in the family plot next to his recently deceased wife and his brother Herschel, killed in the 1906 shootout that occurred near where Gus had met his own fate. It was postponed when, at the instance of Fluker Tarbutton, the Johnson County coroner summoned a jury to investigate the death. The prominence of the parties involved, not to mention the gory details, attracted "several thousand" spectators to the hearing, according to newspaper reports.

Both Charlie Rawlings and Jim Tanner recounted their versions of events. Charlie "told an impressive and plausible story," while Tanner explained how the gun had accidentally discharged, striking Gus in the head. But other and apparently more damning evidence was presented. Most important was the revelation that Gus was well covered by insurance policies payable to either Charlie Rawlings or his struggling bank. Gus's son Fluker contended that his father's death had to be a case of murder. Rather than being shot from a distance, he averred, "the gun was held close to his father's head, this being substantiated by the fact that the man's head was literally blown off." The jury met most of the day, issuing a verdict in the late afternoon stating that there was sufficient reason to believe that Tarbutton's death was a homicide.

Jim Tanner, Hal Hooks, and Louis Stephens were arrested and placed in the Johnson County jail, the two negroes being held as material witnesses. Tanner's arrest warrant specified a charge of murder. A warrant issued for Charlie Rawlings charged him with being an accessory before the fact or, more simply stated, party to a conspiracy to commit murder.

At approximately eight o'clock on Wednesday evening, Johnson County sheriff Lovett Claxton, accompanied by a local Washington County deputy, arrived at Rawlings's home in Sandersville to place him under arrest. The lawman's arrival was somewhat unexpected. Charlie's son Fred and his son-in-law W. A. Wray were present and refused to allow him to be taken into custody until a local attorney could be called to protect the rights of the newly charged defendant. After some negotiation, it was agreed that Charlie would be taken to Wrightsville and held under guard at a local hotel rather than being thrown in jail with Tanner and the negroes. Feelings were running high in Wrightsville. Within the crowd that had gathered for the hearing earlier in the day, there was talk of lynching, prompting Tanner's family to request that extra guards be posted around the county jail.

Gus's funeral was held at eleven in the morning of February 19 at his plantation home, after which a funeral cortege carried his body to Sandersville for burial. It was said to be "the longest seen here in many, many years. A large truck...carried several dozen colored farm tenants from the

Tarbutton plantations." The Wrightsville paper opined that "Mr. Tarbutton was a good man in every sense of the word," not hesitating to milk the event for every lurid detail. It reported,

> Many great streams of the population from five counties carried on to the scene of the death of Mr. Tarbutton and pushed their way to the banks of the Oconee until [they made] a well beaten path and an open route to this dismal, secluded spot that marks the fate of Johnson's beloved citizen. All day long they poured back there and took it all in and hardly a single person left without forming and expressing some opinion as to the cause of this good man's sudden taking off. Ever and anon they came and every day they have gone there and tears fell from the bewildered eyes of hundreds as they took in the awfulness of the situation; let it be an accident or willful murder it is considered awful.

The story went on to question why the test pits were being dug in the first place, hinting that one might be a "snug hole." The *Macon News* took this even farther, unequivocally describing the pit near the death site as "a big grave," the unstated implication being it had been dug to hide Tarbutton's body.

Despite the *Wrightsville Headlight*'s assertion that "our people are, and have been, cool and level-headed all the while, regardless of wild reports to the contrary," Sheriff Claxton decided that action was needed to protect the prisoners' lives. Rawlings was transferred to the Emanuel County jail some twenty-seven miles away in Swainsboro, riding unguarded with Claxton in his personal car. Tanner was taken to the sheriff's own house to stay until feelings subsided.

The killing—some were now beginning to refer to it as "murder"—and the arrest of "a member of one of the most prominent families in middle Georgia," earned front-page headlines across the state. Assured of his innocence, Charlie did not hesitate in giving a statement to the reporters who tracked him down at the Emanuel County jail. He said his heart was crushed because he was charged with planning the death of someone he had viewed almost as a son. "Why, I raised the boy. I started him off in life. I loved him as my own child and I have stood by him in fair weather and foul. I spent thousands of dollars on him when he was on trial for murder. Tarbutton knew that in my heart I never had anything but the highest and best feeling for him." He continued, "I am deeply grieved because anybody should think that I would do harm to one whom I have loved as my own child." He concluded by saying, "I am anxious to know what there is against me," obviously not recognizing the significance others placed on the insurance policies. "I am innocent," he said simply.

Jim Tanner gave a public statement to the effect that he had never witnessed any enmity between Tarbutton and Rawlings, observing that "they seemed to be best friends as well as cousins." He allowed that "if Rawlings had ever tried to get him to do a dirty deed for him that he would have slapped [him] in the mouth."

For whatever public statements he might have made, Charlie clearly had reason to worry. Gus Tarbutton had been a popular and respected man in the county where any trial would take place. The Ku Klux Klan was locally powerful and influential and had already shown their displeasure with Charlie in a most gruesome way. There was no real way of knowing who among those chosen as jurymen might be Klan members or subject to Klan influence. And if these facts were not enough, simple public opinion was against him, not to mention the seemingly biased local newspaper coverage. He could only hope that a grand jury would find the facts insufficient to warrant his continued detention. If not, and he were convicted of the crime with which he was charged, he stood a good chance of becoming another victim of "Ol' Sparky," as the state's electric chair had become known. There was only one person he could trust to lead his defense team.

Tom Hardwick had served as one of Georgia's senators from 1914 through 1919, then as governor from 1921 to 1923. He had taken a firm anti-Klan stance on both a national and state level and was soundly defeated in his attempts to win another term as senator in 1922 and again in 1924, something for which the Klan proudly took credit. After his second defeat he retired from politics, announcing in late January 1925 that he was opening a law practice in Dublin. There was no doubt that he was the one to lead the defense. Hardwick met first with his client and friend at the hotel in Wrightsville the afternoon after Charlie's arrest. Afterward, neither would give a statement to the reporters who were following the events closely.

The commitment hearing, a proceeding before justices of the peace designed to review the preliminary evidence and decide if there were sufficient reasons to hold the accused under arrest, was scheduled for Friday, February 27. The delay gave both sides time to build a legal team and gather evidence. The paper predicted "a thousand people" at the courthouse to hear the details of the case. The evidence against Rawlings and Tanner was the same, but their initial hearings were to be held separately. The same group of lawyers would defend both men. In addition to Hardwick, Charlie hired attorneys from the two leading firms in Sandersville, plus a local attorney from Wrightsville, a relative of the sheriff.

The state's case against the accused was to be prosecuted by Fred Kea, the local solicitor. Kea was originally from

Johnson County but had practiced law in Dublin for years, in addition to having served two terms as state senator. Middle-aged and seeking a more comfortable position, he had run and been elected in the Georgia Democratic White Primary in September the preceding year. In an endorsement, the *Headlight* had described him as "a brilliant and capable member of the bar." He described himself as "a total abstainer" while seeking the backing of the Women's Christian Temperance Union.

As was the custom of the day, injured parties were allowed to hire additional private attorneys to act in the role of co-prosecutors in criminal cases. For Fluker Tarbutton, much was riding on the outcome of the proceedings. In addition to seeking justice for what he considered the murder of his father, there were the twin issues of ownership of thousands of acres of land, plus hundreds of thousands of dollars in potential insurance settlements. As primary co-counsel, Fluker retained J. L. Kent, a well-connected local state court judge. Two other prominent attorneys, one each from Wrightsville and Sandersville, were hired to assist Kea and Kent. The accused bided their time in jail while the attorneys prepared their cases. News reports predicted, "This promises to be one of the most bitter criminal trials in the annals of Georgia courts, with each side fighting every inch of the way."

Charlie Rawlings's hearing began promptly at 10:00 AM on Friday, February 27, before three local men sworn as justices of the peace. In the days after arrests of the accused, rumors had begun to circulate about the existence of a "surprise witness" for the state, adding an air of suspense to the carnival-like mood surrounding the proceedings. A throng estimated to be 700 persons—at least 200 of whom were women—jostled for standing room in the crowded courtroom. After a prayer by a local Baptist minister for divine guidance, the state opened with testimony from Hal Hooks, Charlie's chauffeur. By now the details of the case were well known, having been recounted over and over in local newspapers and in daily conversations on the street. Hooks testified that he heard the gunshot, then ran to the scene to find Charlie "crying and wringing his hands" over Gus's lifeless form. He rushed to the nearest farmhouse where he procured a quilt in which the men wrapped the body to take it home.[1] During the testimony, Rawlings "openly wept...and seemed deeply affected by Hooks's recital of the scenes leading up to the killing of his first cousin."

Other witnesses confirmed Hooks's account. A geologist testified that the samples of bauxite ore said to come from the Ring Jaw property had come from elsewhere, but this was disputed by Tarbutton's bookkeeper. On the other hand, two local physicians gave their opinion that the killing could not have occurred as described by Tanner as the angle of the head wound would have been different. Finally, the long-anticipated surprise witness, a man named Noah Covington, was called to the stand.

Covington, a seventy-year-old farm laborer, testified that he had in fact been on Ring Jaw Bluff that day, and—unseen by the participants in the drama—had witnessed the actual killing. He testified that he had decided to take up commercial fishing and had spent the day "prospecting" along the banks of the Oconee looking for "good places to fish." He said he had just stopped at a small spring to get a drink of water when he heard voices and saw the three men—Tarbutton, Tanner, and

---

[1] To quote the *Progress*'s account, "Hooks was asked if he was frightened by the dead body and answered, 'Yas sah. I shore was a skeered nigger.' This brought the first gale of laughter to the court spectators and lawyers" (4 March 1925).

Rawlings—approaching. As he watched, less than a hundred feet away and unseen by the men, he observed Tanner raise the shotgun to his shoulder and deliberately shoot Tarbutton in the head. Fearing for his life, he fled toward home, walking some twenty miles through the night.

Two days after the killing, overcome by guilt at not revealing what he knew, Covington had posted an unsigned letter to Sheriff Claxton stating that an unnamed witness had observed the killing. Several days later, Covington appeared at the sheriff's office to confess that he was that man and was willing to testify in court as to the true details of Tarbutton's death. His account sounded plausible and seemed to fit exactly with the state's theory about the actual events that took place on Ring Jaw Bluff.

On cross-examination by the defense, Covington's credibility seemed less persuasive. He acknowledged that he had served time on the chain gang for making illicit whiskey. He reluctantly admitted that a few weeks earlier he had stood at the train depot in Bartow soliciting donations, falsely posing as a reformed convict who had served prison time for murder in Mississippi and was now trying to lead an honest and upright life.

Finally, as if the more than $200,000 in insurance on Tarbutton's life was not enough, the state introduced evidence that Rawlings and the Citizens Bank were being sued by the War Finance Corporation for unpaid debts in the amount of $79,000. This additional revelation that Charlie Rawlings was in deep financial straits would surely be enough to make a strong circumstantial case for premeditated murder. With Covington's eyewitness account, the soundness of the state's case seemed certain.

After an overnight adjournment, the defense opened their case with the surprising statement that their only witness would be Charlie Rawlings himself. Having been portrayed thus far as a feeble old man[2] incapable of harming anyone, he was seated in a chair directly in front of the justices and began his testimony "in a low but clear voice:" "Gentlemen: I don't know exactly what to say...." Once again he recited his version of the facts, sobbing and muttering "in a half broken voice, 'I raised Gus Tarbutton as if he were my own son.'" He admitted to owing "a good deal of money," stating the insurance policies "were taken out to help my credit and to help Mr. Tarbutton's credit."

The two sides presented their closing arguments, the prosecution first, followed by the defense. Kea spoke for the state, giving "one of the best speeches ever delivered in the courthouse here in the trial of any case," as assessed by the local newspaper editor, clearly one of his fans.[3] Ex-governor Hardwick then spoke for an hour and a half, making a "brilliant plea" for the innocence of his client. His argument, punctuated by dramatic pauses and a "thundering voice," was described by the Sandersville paper—supportive of the defense—as "one of the most dramatic ever heard in the courthouse here." He closed with a moving "plea for liberty for crippled old man Rawlings." Despite the weight of Hardwick's

---

[2] Various press reports described Rawlings as suffering from "arthritis," "partial paralysis," the ravages of "typhoid," and being "partly an invalid." It is not unreasonable to think many of these descriptions were designed to elicit sympathy on the part of the court as they appear to be inconsistent with other reports of his health both before and after the Tarbutton killing and the court proceedings that followed.

[3] *Wrightsville Headlight*, 5 March 1925.

oratory, the consensus among those present held that the prisoner would be bound over for trial.

The justices retired to deliberate the matter, returning less than fifteen minutes later to hand their written decision to Solicitor Fred Kea. Kea glanced at the statement, evidently shocked. He stammered, then read, "It is ordered that the said C. G. Rawlings be released from custody. This February 28, 1925." Charlie wept as a crowd of friends and supporters surrounded the defense table. On the other side of the courtroom, Fluker Tarbutton's attorneys plotted their next move.

24

The Problem Witness

Noah Covington was a problem. For all the commotion, notoriety, and speculation surrounding the death of Gus Tarbutton, the state's case against Tanner and Rawlings was relatively weak. There was little doubt that Charlie Rawlings was deeply in debt, but so were many others in similar situations across the agricultural South. It was true that Gus Tarbutton's life was insured, but he too was in debt, and insurance coverage was a legitimate option to help his family and business partners meet his obligations should he come to an untimely end. Even the facts and circumstances of Gus's death were not for the most part in dispute. The one fundamental question that had to be answered was this: was the shotgun that killed Gus Tarbutton under the control of Jim Tanner or not? Covington said it was.

If the state could somehow prove that Tanner deliberately shot Tarbutton, the next problem would be his motive. From the evidence presented in the preliminary hearings, he would seem to have little reason to want him dead. But Jim Tanner was an employee of a man who might—Charlie Rawlings. It would then fall on the state to prove that Rawlings and Tanner had developed an elaborate conspiracy to stage Tarbutton's "accidental" death, something that would realistically require leaps of faith on the part of any unbiased jury. Without an eyewitness, the case would have to be decided on circumstantial evidence. And with the best legal team that money could buy, it was not unreasonable to think that both

Tanner and Rawlings stood a good chance of being acquitted of all charges. Covington was that eyewitness, the missing link in the otherwise tenuous chain of evidence.

But there were larger, unspoken considerations. Justice aside, there were many who would stand to gain by Charlie Rawlings being convicted of murder. While he may have been deeply in debt, he was still a wealthy man and one of largest landowners in two counties. He owned controlling interest in a bank, a railroad, and various businesses. All of his assets would likely come up for sale at steep discounts should he be sentenced to prison or, worse, to the electric chair. For Fluker Tarbutton, Charlie's conviction would allow him to dispute the ownership of his father's plantation, not to mention the likelihood of his collecting on insurance policies whose proceeds had been assigned to cover debt to Charlie or his bank. For the insurance companies, whose total exposure would eventually be revealed to be in excess of $300,000, conviction would obviate the need to pay double indemnity clauses for accidental death, and possibly allow them to completely deny payment if a firm case for conspiracy could be established. Given these considerations, the testimony of a witness like Noah Covington was something of value, something on which a price could be placed.

The preliminary hearing for Jim Tanner, still being held in jail without bail, was scheduled for Wednesday, March 4. After the verdict freeing Rawlings, Solicitor Kea announced that he would be presenting the matter to the grand jury that was to meet on March 16, the implication being that while the justices may have freed one of the accused, there would still be another opportunity to place him back in custody. The *Macon News* reported a rumor that "three new justices of the peace will be secured to hear the evidence" against Tanner. The hearing hadn't turned out as planned, so a change of citizen-jurists might yield a more favorable result for the state. It was announced that Tanner's legal team would be the same as that for Rawlings, but Tom Hardwick would act as an advisor and observer instead of directly participating in court. Meanwhile, Charlie Rawlings arrived home in Sandersville late in the afternoon to be greeted by a crowd of supporters and wellwishers.

Tanner's hearing began with Judge J. L. Kent, speaking for the state, objecting to the same thee justices presiding over the case. He contended, "they were disqualified after having heard previous testimony in the Rawlings case." After a brief recess during which the justices conferred in private, they agreed to step down and allow others to preside over the hearing. The sheriff, charged with appointing justices of the peace, initially chose another prominent local citizen to preside, but he was quickly removed on objection of the defense. A second man suitable to both sides was then appointed, but he refused to serve alone and requested that two other justices be appointed. After a recess of several hours during which two others willing to serve as justices were found, the hearing got under way in the early afternoon.

The state's case was essentially the same as that presented against Charlie Rawlings, with Noah Covington again giving his damning testimony. This time he added that he was "about thirty yards" from the accused when the killing took place in case there was any doubt about his being near enough to observe exactly what happened. In the several days since the earlier hearing, the defense had done their homework, seeking out testimony to destroy the credibility of the state's star witness. A man named Tyler Faulkner said he had spoken with Covington two days after Tarbutton's killing, telling him about what happened. Covington allegedly said that was the first he had heard of it. A farmer, Otis Kendall, testified that about three o'clock on the afternoon of the killing he had seen Covington pass his house, some fifteen miles distant from Ring Jaw Bluff. Other witnesses were called to impugn Covington's character. In addition to the past sins revealed at the Rawlings hearing, he was forced to admit that he had been tried and acquitted of hog stealing, but earlier had pled guilty to cheating and swindling.

The defense also presented evidence from the county surveyor. He had measured the distances and elevations at the site of the killing and found that it was quite possible that the wound in Tarbutton's head could have been produced if the accident happened as Tanner contended. Another witness demonstrated how Tanner's shotgun could have discharged in the manner described, again supporting the theory of accidental death. Finally Tanner himself spoke to the justices, briefly retelling his story in a "low but clear voice."

After four and a half hours of testimony and two hours of closing arguments, the justices retired to consider their verdict. As in the earlier hearing, it only took them about fifteen minutes to reach a conclusion. Tanner was ordered held without bail pending a grand jury investigation and presumed indictment for capital murder.

The Johnson County Grand Jury met on Monday, March 16, the same day an adjuster for the Prudential Life Insurance Company arrived in Sandersville. By now, the extent of Gus Tarbutton's insurance coverage was becoming clearer. The total amount was said to be some $270,000, part of which was a $50,000 policy carrying double indemnity in case of accidental death. Unless challenged, Prudential and others would be obligated to pay some $320,000 to the policies' beneficiaries. Of this amount, "a very small part" was payable to the estate of

Gus Tarbutton, $53,000 to the Citizens Bank, and the remainder "to the surviving partner of the firm of Rawlings & Tarbutton, viz., Mr. C. G. Rawlings." The adjuster said that Rawlings's creditors had already filed garnishment levies against the insurance proceeds.

On March 17, the grand jury issued true bills for a charge of murder against Tanner and Rawlings. The indictments were not unexpected. Overseeing the jury was District Judge R. Earl Camp, who—like Solicitor Kea—had been elected in the Democratic White Primary some six months earlier. His candidacy had garnered the endorsement of the *Headlight*, which described him as "one of the most prominent and successful lawyers in the Dublin judicial circuit." The paper, pleased with the grand jury's indictments, now praised Camp's charge to the jury, noting, "He is starting off well in the official duties of the presiding Jurist of this Circuit." Camp had been the same attorney who some years earlier had represented the Brooks family in their lawsuit alleging fraud by Rawlings in an attempt to gain ownership of the family's land. His role as presiding judge now portended ominous events.

An arrest warrant was issued for Charlie Rawlings, but he was nowhere to be found. One report suggested that he had left town the preceding weekend on a "business trip," possibly to North Carolina. The *Charlotte Observer*, joining the search for the fugitive, called Charlie's daughter's home in Monroe, North Carolina, only to be told that his whereabouts were unknown. Charlie's attorneys refused to confirm or deny if they were aware of their client's location, but assured the Johnson County sheriff that he would appear as scheduled for the forthcoming jury trial, now scheduled for March 23. Hardwick commented "that Rawlings was in such bad health that he wanted to get all the rest possible before he went to trial." Meanwhile, both the prosecution and the defense searched for witnesses and prepared for the coming court battles.

A Battle Hard Fought

The trial of Charlie Rawlings and Jim Tanner began on Monday morning, March 23, one day short of five weeks after Gus Tarbutton's death. The previous proceedings—the coroner's jury, the commitment hearings, the grand jury—had offered both sides chances to present their stories, hear the evidence, explore the witnesses, and gauge the strength of the other's case. Whether the attorneys for the defense chose to admit it publicly or not, they knew that the road would eventually lead to a jury trial once the coroner had rendered a verdict of possible homicide. This was it. The next days (and, as it would turn out, the next months) would determine whether two men would continue on with their lives if found innocent or, if convicted, face the Odyssean prospects of life in prison or the electric chair.

The transcript of the trial still exists, an 859-page, laboriously typed document, now yellow and crumbling with age. Full of misspellings and colloquialisms, it faithfully reproduces the cadence of early twentieth-century Southern dialect, where "helped" was "hoped,"[1] and walking was traveling "afoot." It

---

[1] Many of the nuances that make southern dialectical speech unique are descended from the voice patterns of the early immigrants from northern England and Scotland. The word "help," which in more modern times has morphed into a so-called "weak verb" with regular conjugations, was formerly (in Middle English) an irregular verb whose simple past tense was "holp," pronounced similarly to "hope." This in turn has become "hoped."

captures the often-heated exchanges between attorneys and the judge, and reveals social statements when blacks are referenced in open court as "darkies," and persons of a certain age awarded the generic honorific of "uncle." The presence of an audience of curious spectators is reflected by such notations as "Demonstration in the Audience," following a controversial statement by a witness, which in turn would elicit a rebuke from the judge and a threat to clear the courtroom.[2]

With Judge R. Earl Camp presiding, the trial formally got under way in early afternoon after several hours of jury selection. Both sides used their strikes freely, finally agreeing on a panel of twelve men, eleven of whom were farmers and a twelfth who gave his occupation as "shingle mill operator." Testimony was heard for the remainder of the day, then through Tuesday, Wednesday, and into Thursday morning, after which both sides gave lengthy closing arguments.

Although Rawlings and Tanner had been jointly indicted on the basis of the same circumstances and facts in evidence, the proceedings began with a motion from the defense for separate trials. Attorneys for the prosecution readily agreed, electing to try Tanner first. It was a logical choice. While he may have been the person whose gun killed Tarbutton, there was little doubt that the ultimate goal was to convict the man they considered responsible for the alleged conspiracy, Charlie Rawlings. The direct evidence was strongest against Tanner, therefore winning a conviction against him would be somewhat easier. And without Tanner's conviction, the case against Rawlings would become moot. On the other side, by allowing Tanner to be tried first, the defense team could know exactly what to expect in terms of evidence and witnesses in any

---

[2] Transcript provided by Donald Smith of Wrightsville.

subsequent trial of Rawlings. He, after all, was the one who was paying their legal fees.

Solicitor Fred Kea and J. L. Kent were the lead attorneys for the prosecution, while A. Willis Evans became the voice of the defense. Tom Hardwick remained in the courtroom, interjecting only occasionally on points of law. He planned to take the lead himself at Rawlings's trial, and this would give him an opportunity to observe the state's case. As the prosecution built their case for conspiracy, Jim Tanner—the poor illiterate farm overseer on trial for his life—was scarcely mentioned as testimony focused on Charlie Rawlings and his business relationship with Gus Tarbutton. For example, after one exchange between attorneys, the judge felt obligated to remind the prosecution's attorney that "Rawlings is not on trial," to which he received the reply, "He is charged with the same offense." The prosecution was allowed to continue, with Judge Camp giving broad latitude as to the admissibility of evidence and statements, all based on the state's attempt to establish a pattern of conspiracy.

The first witness to testify was Lewis Stephens, who again recounted in general terms the now-familiar events surrounding Gus Tarbutton's death. Hal Hooks was not called to testify, possibly because of his close association with Charlie Rawlings. The first witnesses to give substantive testimony were two physicians who had examined the body as part of the coroner's jury. Both agreed that Tarbutton had been shot at close range, "not over ten or twelve inches," according to one, but neither saw powder burns. The undertaker who embalmed the body said he thought he did, however, with all parties agreeing on the fact that the blast seemed to have gone directly though his head from the back to the front.

Next, in order to prove a conspiracy, the state called Claude Brown, who testified that several months earlier Jim Tanner had confided to him that "Rawlings wants me to do something that means big money for [him]," indicating he was reluctant to comply with his employer's request. The matter seemed to involve insurance, with the state implying that Tarbutton's murder had been plotted for some time.

Claude was the son of H. T. Brown, the night watchman and former employee of Charlie Rawlings who had confessed to arson in the burning of the oil mill in May 1921. As the defense was able to show on cross-examination and with later witnesses, following Charlie's acquittal and the state's failure to prove arson in 1922, he had filed suit again the insurance companies, hoping to collect on the policies. Tanner had been sent as an emissary to Claude, whom it was hoped could talk his father into supporting the suit. Claude, bitter at his father's disgrace, had been heard to say now that "they had old Charlie up and I hope they will break his god damned neck. I don't know anything to tell on him but I wish I did." Brown denied making the statements, later presenting testimony from Gus Tarbutton's brother-in-law[3] to substantiate his good character.

Next was Noah Covington, the star witness and linchpin of the state's case. While dramatic—and, if true, devastating to the defense's case—Covington's account of the incident was generic at best. The "facts" that he testified to were, in essence, public knowledge. While he said that he had witnessed the killing, so could anyone else with the boldness to testify under oath. Both the defense and the prosecution recognized this weakness, the former determined to exploit it and the latter determined to strengthen it. Again, Covington described

---

[3] Dr. T. L. Harris, a self-described "Minister of the Gospel," lawyer, doctor of medicine, and architect.

Tanner's actions, stating, "He looked around that way toward Rawlings, which was behind him, then throwed the gun[4] up and shot Tarbutton right in the back of the head."

In the previous proceedings, Covington had said he then fled toward home, walking overnight more than twenty miles,[5] not speaking to anyone on the way. Now he recalled that he had run into "an old darky," a man named Harry Brown, who was skinning a coon. It was established that the shooting took place at approximately 5:15 in the afternoon. Terrified, Covington swore he ran "four or five miles" through the river swamp before emerging on a road and speaking with Brown. Brown was later called and confirmed that he had indeed seen and exchanged pleasantries with Covington, noting the time to be specifically "between sunset and dark."

On February 17, 1925, sunset was at 6:22 PM with twilight lasting about twenty-five minutes,[6] establishing with some precision the time Covington would have arrived at Brown's house, located on a straight line about six miles from Ring Jaw Bluff. The problem was that Covington said he had fled down the river, making the distance he would have actually traveled some fifteen miles in about an hour, a speed nearing that of Roger Bannister, who first shattered the four-minute-mile record in 1954. On a practical basis, one would do well to cover a mile's distance in an hour through the treacherous river swamp.

---

[4] In subsequent testimony, the gun was described as a double-barreled, hammerless Stevens shotgun, purchased originally by Tanner's son at C. A. Adams store in Sandersville for $27.90. The gauge was not given, but the gun was loaded with No. 5 shot, appropriate for snakes and small game.

[5] Testimony would establish the more exact distance to be between twenty-seven and twenty-eight miles.

[6] United States Naval Observatory website.

Several days after the killing, Covington said he had gone to the sheriff to confess that he had been an unseen observer and was willing to testify in court. The first person the sheriff contacted was Fluker Tarbutton. Within a few days, Covington was living on Tarbutton's place. He also admitted returning to Ring Jaw Bluff on the day prior to Rawlings's commitment hearing in the company of several men, including Ben Tarbutton, manager of the Sandersville Railroad and first cousin to both Gus Tarbutton and Charlie Rawlings.

Testimony was next heard about the insurance on Tarbutton's life. There were a number of policies, at least two of them carrying double indemnity clauses. The total payout in case of accidental death would have been approximately $320,000. Two witnesses again confirmed that Charlie Rawlings had asked about the policies shortly after the killing. Other witnesses, including Charlie's son-in-law W. A. Wray, revealed that most of this amount would have gone to Tarbutton's estate. The Citizens Bank was owed only between $34,000 and $35,000, and Gus's indebtedness to Charlie was said to be $90,000, the amount loaned after the disastrous crop year of 1921.

In furtherance of the conspiracy theory, several witnesses for the state suggested that the bauxite-containing rock samples allegedly from Ring Jaw Bluff might have been collected elsewhere, specifically from a bauxite mine in Wilkinson County that Rawlings and others had visited some months earlier.

The state's final major witness was Fluker Tarbutton, whose testimony was both hostile and bitter. Denying the extent of his father's business relationship with Charlie, he averred, "There has never been a partnership of Tarbutton and

Rawlings." He continued, "My father always done the work and Rawlings got half of it."

The defense began their presentation on the afternoon of the second day of the trial, offering a string of witnesses to discredit the character of Noah Covington. Otis Coleman, a former sheriff of Emanuel County, testified that his reputation was "bad." Otis's brother, Elisha Coleman, had once been jailed in Treutlen County, accused of a murder that he contended was an accident. Elisha stated that Covington had visited him in jail, where "He wanted me to hire him to swear me out." Coleman said, "I asked him what he could swear, what did he know, and he said he didn't know anything, but if I would pay him he would know something." A physician testified that Covington had spent seventeen years as "a dope fiend" until the Harrison Narcotic Act had cut off his access to morphine. Other witnesses testified as to how Covington had swindled money in a nonexistent timber transaction.

Faced with a withering attack on his witness's character, Solicitor Kea turned to the tactic that indeed Covington may at one time have been of low moral character, but he had now reformed. To one witness, who swore he would not believe anything Covington said under oath, Kea posed the following question: "I will ask you this, if a man is black today, so far as sin is concerned, and tomorrow is made as white as snow,[7] or do you deny the Divinity of Christ? I will ask you that first, do you deny the Divinity of Christ?" Willis Evans, the defense attorney started to object, but Kea continued, "Do you believe that a man can be as black as smut today, so far as sin is concerned, and be made as white as snow tomorrow?"

"Yes, sir," the witness answered.

---

[7] The biblical references to "as white as snow" come from Isaiah 1:16 and Psalm 51:7.

"Do you deny the Divinity of Christ?" Kea probed again.

"No, sir, I don't."

"And do you believe a man can be as black as smut today and be as white as snow tomorrow?" Kea asked once again.

"Yes, sir."

Having made his point, Kea then asked, "Do you know whether Noah Covington has been forgiven or not?"

The witness, now trapped by the theological argument replied, "No, sir, if he has, it's been lately."

When a later witness disparaged Covington's character because of his involvement with liquor, Kea observed, "If every man that has had whiskey in his possession in the last twelve months was prosecuted, about two-thirds of us would be in the chain gang, wouldn't we?" In response, the judge sustained the defense's objection.

The defense's attack on Covington continued. Four seemingly reliable and disinterested witnesses stated they had seen him near his home some twenty-seven or twenty-eight miles away on the afternoon of the day he was supposedly looking for places to fish near Ring Jaw Bluff. Another witness said that he'd spoken to Covington about Tarbutton's death two days after it happened. Covington seemed surprised, saying it was the first he had heard of it. He then went on to say that Gus's death was divine retribution for his escape from being charged with Tyre's murder in 1906.

Their witness battered, the state brought in Jesse Covington, Noah's son. It was alleged that Noah had spent the Monday night prior to the day of the killing with his son, something that directly contradicted the witnesses who had placed him elsewhere that day. Jesse testified that indeed his father had been with him and had gone fishing the next day as he had testified. His testimony was offset by the absence of another of

Noah Covington's children, Mary Redfirm, who was living
with her brother at the time and would also have been able to
confirm her father's story. She had been subpoenaed but was
nowhere to be found, having "disappeared."

The defense's final argument involved the lay of the land
at Ring Jaw Bluff and the angle at which Gus Tarbutton had
been shot. The county surveyor had made a plat of the site of
the killing, indicating a drop of about twenty-five inches between where Tanner and Tarbutton were said to have been
standing. Testimony was presented that if Tanner had shoul-
dered the gun and fired it as Covington described, the shot
would have gone over Tarbutton's head. On the other hand, if
Tanner had fallen and the gun fired from a lower elevation, the
nature and angle of the wound would fit with Tanner's story.

Conflicting testimony was now given as to the exact
placement of shooter and victim. The county coroner, who had
earlier indicated to the surveyor that a stake driven into the
ground[8] represented where Tarbutton was standing when he
was shot, now said the stake marked where *his head* had lain
after he fell forward. This had the effect of placing Tarbutton
some six feet closer to Tanner at the time of the shooting, a
seeming Procrustean adjustment of earlier facts in evidence.
The sides argued back and forth over the point, neither achieving a clear advantage but managing in the process to so con-
fuse the issue that most listeners would be uncertain whom to
believe.

As was the standard of the day, the defendant was
allowed to make a non-sworn statement to the court with the
understanding that he would not be subject to questioning or
cross-examination. In a quiet, plaintive way, Tanner retold the

---

[8] Referred to as a "stob," a southern dialectal word directly
descended from Middle English.

William Rawlings

events of February 17, explaining, "When this thing happened or occurred, I wouldn't have had it to happen or occur for the whole world. I am just as innocent as a baby. I am just as sorry as can be. Me and him were the best of friends."

By mid-morning on Thursday, March 24, both sides had completed their presentations. Judge Camp allotted six hours for closing arguments. For the prosecution, Kea focused on Noah Covington as an eyewitness, calling on the jury for a conviction in the name of law enforcement "until such awful crimes are stopped." Willis Evans spoke for the defense, calling the basis of the state's case "prejudice and presumption." After being charged by the judge, the jury retired near 6:00 PM to consider their verdict. By 10:30, they had not reached a decision and turned in for the night, under guard.

On Friday, the following day, the jury once again began deliberations, reaching consensus early in the afternoon after a total of more than ten hours of consideration. The *Progress* reported,

> At 2:30 this afternoon a flurry of excitement flashed through the crowd that had been waiting for the jury's report when it was announced that a verdict had been reached and as the twelve men filed into the jury box where they had been confined since Monday, there was a death-like silence as the foreman read the verdict, which carried with it the court's recommendation of mercy. Judge Camp immediately pronounced sentence on Tanner and in a remarkably short time the courthouse was empty.

Mr. J. J. Tanner, former Washington county citizen, who will be given preliminary trial at Wrightsville this morning at 10 o'clock on the charge of murdering Mr. G. A. Tarbutton, planter of Johnson county. Mr. Tanner emphatically contends the killing was purely an accident. This photograph was made in the court house at Wrightsville last Saturday afternoon especially for the Sandersville Progress.

The various trials of Jim Tanner and Charlie Rawlings attracted huge crowds as well as media coverage. Tanner agreed to pose for this photo at his arraignment hearing.

Tanner sat silently as the jury pronounced him guilty and the judge sentenced him to life in prison. His attorneys immediately filed an appeal for a new trial, after which he was taken to the jail in Dublin for "safekeeping" amid new rumors of mob violence. Judge Camp drew the names of seventy-five new jurors to serve as a pool for Charlie Rawlings's trial, now scheduled to begin on Monday morning, March 30. Meanwhile, as the paper noted, "Rawlings is under the care of a physician."[9]

---

[9] *Sandersville Progress*, 1 April 1925.

26

Everything Falls Apart

While Tanner's trial was under way in Wrightsville, Charlie Rawlings's business empire was crumbling around him. On March 24, as he sat observing the trial of his overseer and co-defendant, Charlie was served notice that four separate legal actions totaling $149,882.53 had been filed against him seeking to stop payment of any insurance proceeds he might be due as a result of Gus Tarbutton's death. Under indictment or not, he had gone ahead and filed an affidavit to collect on that portion of the insurance that was due him, the Citizens Bank, and the firm of Rawlings & Tarbutton. The legal actions were probably unnecessary; the insurance companies were unlikely to pay anyway without extended litigation. The suits did solidify his creditors' claims, however, just in case he might be due any money.

The timing of the action was ironic in the sense that on the same day the notices were being served, insurance agents were testifying in court that at least some of the policies on Gus Tarbutton's life had been funded by security deeds given against property rather than paid in cash. Charlie Rawlings, like many in the agricultural South of the mid-1920s, now found himself "land poor." He had plenty in assets—mainly land—but little in hard currency. And what he might have had was being siphoned off by the gaggle of attorneys he had necessarily hired to defend his life.

Charlie's murder conspiracy trial began on Monday morning, March 30, as scheduled. A "tremendous crowd" had gathered as the defendant, "showing evidence of ill health...entered the courtroom supported by two friends, having been brought from the jail in a wheel chair." The trial ended within minutes when Tom Hardwick moved for a change of venue, citing "the violent prejudice" that existed against his client and "the danger of violence" to which he would be exposed. He contended "that his client could not get a fair and impartial trial in Johnson County." After hearing brief arguments from both sides, Judge Camp denied the motion, effectively stopping all action pending appeal before a higher court. Hardwick then filed a motion to release his client on bail.

As the various interested parties schemed and plotted their next moves, the *Sandersville Progress*—in another bit of unintended irony—announced that a well digger near the village of Deepstep in western Washington County had discovered a "valuable deposit of what is believed to be a high grade of bauxite." The article, and another the following week quoting the head of the new Department of Ceramics at Georgia Tech, spoke of "rich veins" and "abundant" quantities of various types of clay in the area, stating, "the mines only await development in order to bring wealth to the owners." Charlie Rawlings, soon to be on trial for his life, was not to be one of them. He remained in jail, his appeal for bail having been denied by Judge Camp.

On April 18, a joint petition was filed in the Washington County Superior Court by several attorneys representing Charlie's creditors, alleging he was in "no condition, physically or mentally, to give attention to his business assets." Judge R. N. Hardeman, the same man who had presided over Charlie's arson trial some three years earlier, "immediately" appointed Lake B. Holt as temporary receiver, later making the position permanent. The court granted Holt $10,000 per year stipend as receiver while giving Rawlings $300 per month during his lifetime. The petition estimated Rawlings's debts as approximately $200,000 and his assets between $700,000 and $1,000,000, primarily land in Washington and Johnson counties. He was insolvent but by no means bankrupt. Holt, described by the *Atlanta Constitution* as "a former business associate" of Charlie's, was empowered to operate the farms in the best interest of the creditors. The total amount of money involved was said to be "the largest sum that has ever been filed in the courts of the county."

On April 21, the court of appeals denied Hardwick's request for a change of venue for Rawlings's trial, citing "no danger of mob violence" in Johnson County. He immediately appealed the matter to the state's supreme court. Charlie remained in jail in Wrightsville, joined by Jim Tanner who had been brought back from Dublin now that local tempers seemed to have cooled.

On April 23, the State Banking Department formally closed the Citizens Bank of Sandersville. Most depositors had withdrawn their funds in the two months since Charlie's arrest; only about $3,000 in deposits—mainly time certificates—remained. Depositors were assured they would be fully reimbursed. Meanwhile, Lake Holt had just completed the takeover of another Washington County bank, merging it and a previous purchase into the rapidly growing Holt Banking Company. The news announcement again extolled him "as one of the best financiers in the state,...recognized in banking circles as one of the most capable bankers." Charlie Rawlings should have considered himself fortunate to have his assets overseen by such a man as Lake Holt.

The squabble continued over how much would be collected from Gus Tarbutton's insurance and who would receive it. Though the majority of the amount would have been credited to his estate even after his debts to the Citizens Bank and Charlie Rawlings were paid, Fluker, as sole heir and administrator, contended that all of it should go to his father's estate. The dispute moved to federal court on April 28 when the Prudential Insurance Company, obligated under the policies for as much as $105,000, filed suit charging Gus Tarbutton himself with fraud based on statements he had made when taking out the policies in which he failed to disclose the fact that he also had other life insurance policies. Incidentally mentioned was the additional allegation that Gus had died as a result of a murder conspiracy, but this in and of itself would not be sufficient for Prudential to deny the claim.

By early May, interest in the case seemed to be waning. For the first time in nearly two and a half months, the *Progress* carried no news item on any aspect of the affair. Rawlings's trial was still scheduled for the June term of superior court, subject of course to a ruling by the supreme court on his motion for a change of venue. Attorneys for the defense labored on, finally obtaining an affidavit from both Jesse Covington and Mary Redfirm, Noah's children, confessing that Noah had in fact *not* spent the night of February 16 in their company, adding one more bit of evidence that the state's eyewitness had fabricated his story. Essentially admitting that he had perjured himself at Tanner's trial, Jesse withdrew his father's alibi. The daughter, Mary, had "disappeared" when subpoenaed because she did not want to lie under oath. As the month drew to a close, this evidence was presented to Judge Camp in a hearing for a new trial for Jim Tanner. The state, faced with the dilemma of having to discredit testimony that was at the heart of their original case, now found reason to present "affidavits tending towards refuting these and impeachment of the witnesses." Judge Camp denied a new trial, sending Tanner back to the Wrightsville jail to wait out further appeals.

Outside of the drama of the court, life went on across the rural landscape. Farmers plowed and chopped and hoed, all the while praying for rain. The economy remained bleak, with bank failures now a common occurrence. In Wrightsville, the Dixie Theatre played a two-showing special of *The Birth of the Invisible Empire*, a seven-reel picture "telling all about the KKK." It featured "55,000 robed Klansmen and Klanswomen and 15,000 robed horses" and was to be accompanied by "special fireworks and busting of bombs in front of [the] theatre." In nearby Laurens County, Representative J. Marion Peacock announced his intention to introduce legislation to outlaw dancing on the Sabbath Day, placing it in the same category as fishing on Sunday. In Atlanta, a grand jury proposed the "return of the lash in disciplining unruly prisoners in the convict camps." Flogging had been banned two years earlier under the anti-Klan administration of Tom Hardwick. The jury felt it "more humane" than the "stocks and dungeons now being used to handle incorrigible prisoners." And some hundreds of miles to the north in Tennessee, John Scopes was indicted by another grand jury on the heretical charge of teaching evolution in the public schools.

On June 15, Fluker Tarbutton filed a $250,000 civil suit against Jim Tanner and Charlie Rawlings over the death of his father, said to be the largest such action ever filed in the county. The defendants were served notice in jail. Rawlings's trial was still scheduled to begin a week later, but the date was becoming increasingly uncertain as the Georgia Supreme Court had not yet rendered a decision on his request for a change of venue. The local paper advised those "who are interested in any way in the trial" to be present, just in case. Another large audience seemed certain.

The scheduled trial date came and went without word from Atlanta. With the June term of court drawing to a close, Judge Camp rescheduled the trial for August 17, six months to the day after Gus Tarbutton's death. Rawlings was said to be "whiling away the time in the jail and has for his companionship his Bible and Jim Tanner, his former overseer who constantly aids and converses with him," according to Sheriff Lovett J. Claxton. The sheriff noted "that Rawlings takes a lot of time reading his Bible," and that "the defendants are said to be getting along pretty well in their close environment." The court continued to consider Tanner's request for a new trial.

On July 10, the state Supreme Court denied Rawlings's request for a change of venue, affirming the court of appeals's decision that a fair trial was possible in Johnson County. Meanwhile, in tiny Dayton, Tennessee—a town not dissimilar to Wrightsville—the sides assembled for the opening day of the trial of John Scopes, charged with violation of the Butler Act that specifically forbade instructors in any public or private school in the state from teaching "any theory that denies the Story of Divine Creation of man as taught in the Bible."

27

I'm Not Guilty, Of Course

As the dog days of July turned into the heat of early August, Charlie Rawlings and Jim Tanner settled into the routine of jail life. They shared their new accommodations with several other prisoners, some awaiting trial and others serving out their time locally. Charlie, the man with the money, improved the otherwise dreary prison fare by buying the food and having one of the other men prepare it for the group. Among the miscellaneous prisoners was a farmer named Ray Huie, someone who was to play a major role in Charlie's upcoming trial.

Meanwhile in Sandersville, the mid-summer doldrums led the editor of the *Progress* to complain that "local news is hard to find," lamenting that "the noise of an occasional lumber truck is about all there is to be heard." He urged readers to report "anything out of the ordinary." His request was richly rewarded when the story of a widowed mother of thirteen children being gored to death by a cow came over the news wires, earning a prominent spot in the paper because of the peculiar nature of her demise. In Tennessee, a deeply divided jury found John Scopes guilty of teaching evolution. William Jennings Bryan, ex-presidential candidate, Fundamentalist Christian, and victorious lawyer for the prosecution in the case, died in his sleep during an afternoon nap a few days later. The *Wrightsville Headlight*, in a front-page obituary, noted "he had been preparing to launch a national drive against the teaching of evolution in the public schools of the United States." The editor praised him as "one of the brightest men America has ever produced."

On August 17, the parties once again assembled at the Johnson County courthouse to begin Charlie Rawlings's trial. The weather had been oppressive, with temperatures running 100 degrees and above across the South. The crowds, though still large by comparison to other trials, were smaller this time. One of the local papers observed, "Farmers are busy and interest in the case is waning."[1] Another reported, "There has been plenty of room at the courthouse," citing the cotton harvest season which was now in progress.[2]

Both Charlie Rawlings and Jim Tanner were in court. Tanner, already facing life in prison, was described as having "a worried and hopeless appearance." Charlie, on the other hand, accompanied by ex-Governor Hardwick and the six other attorneys of his defense team, was said to "look fit despite his age and infirmities."[3] His widely respected brother, Dr. William Rawlings, was in court for much of the trial, at times sitting beside the defendant. On the opposite side of the courtroom, Fluker Tarbutton, accompanied by "his pretty young wife," sat at the prosecution's table with Solicitor Fred Kea and the four "special attorneys" he had hired to assist the state's case.

The trial opened with a prayer by a local minister, followed by the formal statement of the charges against the defendant and the request that he restate his plea. In a steady

---

[1] Ibid., 19 August 1925.

[2] *Wrightsville Headlight*, 20 August 1925.

[3] One news report said he was "slightly crippled" and "suffering from locomotor ataxia," a term surely supplied by Charlie's attorneys (*Sandersville Progress*, 19 August 1925).

voice, Charlie replied, "I'm not guilty, of course."[4] The remainder of first day of the trial was taken up with jury selection and contentious arguments between the judge and attorneys for both sides. By the afternoon of the second day, a twelve-man jury had been empanelled, all of whom were farmers.

During the midday break on the second day, Solicitor Kea confided to a reporter for the *Macon Telegraph* that he had found "new and startling evidence against Charles G. Rawlings." "I have new evidence that will show Rawlings and Tanner plotted to kill Tarbutton for his insurance," he stated. "This testimony will conclusively prove this plot to the jury." He refused to give further details.

Once again, the same witnesses who had testified in previous court proceedings gave their evidence and accounts of events as they recalled them. The prosecution, in a further attempt to prove the shooting was deliberate, had deputies demonstrate in the courtroom how Tanner's shotgun could not be made to fire accidentally, even when "thrown violently against the ground."

Late on the afternoon of the third day, Noah Covington took the stand. This time he was more precise in his allegations, stating, "I watched Tanner place his gun to his shoulder, and take deliberate aim at Tarbutton and fire." Moreover, his story of how he had observed the shooting had changed somewhat, with new details added to his testimony. The following morning Covington underwent a "grueling" cross-examination by Tom Hardwick, who for three hours "grilled" him on every detail of his account. The reporter for the *Atlanta Constitution*

---

[4] Quoted in the *Wrightsville Headlight*, 20 August 1925. Other news reporters heard his reply as "Why, not guilty, you know" (*Sandersville Progress*, 19 August 1925).

noted, "Covington retained remarkable composure during the questioning and in the main, his story was unshaken."

Following Covington's cross-examination, the state introduced their surprise witness, Ray Huie.[5] Huie was a farmer from Laurens County who ended up in the Johnson County jail with Charlie and Jim Tanner over the summer of 1925 on a charge of larceny after trust. He had been convicted and sentenced to the chain gang. He testified,

> I heard Tanner tell Rawlings that he was not doing what he promised to do, and Rawlings told Tanner that the insurance money was tied up in court, but as quick as it was got out of court he would do what he promised to do. I heard Tanner tell Rawlings that Noah Covington must have been where he said he was, or he could not have told such a straight tale as he told, and Rawlings said that was bought evidence, and then Tanner said, "I wish I hadn't had anything to do with it," but before I heard Tanner say he wished he hadn't had anything to do with it, I heard someone sniff, and when I came out of my cell there was tears in Tanner's face.[6]

Satisfied that Huie's statement was sufficient to prove conspiracy, the state rested their case.

In opening the defense's arguments, Hardwick made a surprise announcement that he would present no witnesses, only the statement of the defendant, Charlie Rawlings. Charlie chose to sit not on the witness stand but in a chair directly in front of the jury. In an earnest soliloquy, sometimes breaking down and weeping, he described how Gus had come to live with his family when he was young, and how he and his

---

[5] Huie's name is variously spelled (and presumably misspelled) several ways in written accounts. I use here the spelling taken from an appeal decision by the Georgia Supreme Court.

[6] *Rawlings v. State* (1926).

cousin had gone into business together after the killing of
Hershel Tarbutton in 1906. "There had never been any
disagreement with him on my part. I introduced him to the
lady he married. We were close together and couldn't have
been any closer together than we were." He said, "I had rather
my own son got killed as he. It is the most ridiculous thing that
ever happened to think of my having anything to do with his
death." As to Huie's statement, Charlie said simply that he was
lying. He had never discussed the case while in jail with
Tanner "because there was nothing to discuss." The *Headlight*,
clearly in the camp of the prosecution, was dismissive of
Charlie's statement, saying only, "His story was about the
same, only longer...."

The defense rested their case and the closing arguments
began. Attorneys for the state spoke for two hours Thursday
afternoon, continuing for nearly two more hours the following
morning. When it was Hardwick's turn, he "savagely"
attacked the state's case, speaking for nearly two hours and
alleging a "conspiracy of the prosecution to accomplish the
conviction of Rawlings by bought testimony." Referring
directly to Fluker Tarbutton, he charged that the motive behind
the state's prosecution of his client was the desire by "by
relatives of Tarbutton" to retain the dead man's entire
insurance proceeds for themselves.

After six hours of deliberation, the jury found the
defendant guilty of murder, with a recommendation of mercy.
Charlie showed no visible emotion as the verdict was read.
Judge Camp immediately sentenced him to life in prison.
Hardwick filed an appeal for a new trial. On the same day, the
Ku Klux Klan announced its annual meeting of Grand Dragons
to be held near Columbus, Georgia. The object of the year's

convention would be to organize "a drive to save America from a pagan civilization—to return the church to Christ."

28

Aftermath

With the trials over and the alleged conspirators now branded as convicted murderers, the once-sensational Tarbutton killing became old news. As temperatures cooled and September became October, attention turned to the cotton harvest and the annual county fairs that had become a staple of the fall season. Meanwhile, Jim Tanner and Charlie Rawlings sat quietly in the Johnson County jail, clinging to whatever glimmer of hope the appeals process might offer.

In mid-October came the unexpected announcement that the Georgia Supreme Court had granted Tanner's request for a new trial. In setting aside his conviction, the court cited Judge Camp's failure to exclude from evidence statements allegedly made by Charlie Rawlings, Tanner's co-defendant. Specifically, these were Charlie's inquiries about Gus Tarbutton's insurance policies made shortly after the killing, ironically the same statements that seemed to have precipitated suspicion that the death may have been more than a simple accident. The *Wrightsville Headlight*, clearly convinced of Tanner's guilt, commented that the grounds for the reversal were "strictly technical," the implication being that this impediment to his eventual conviction would be overcome in any subsequent trial.

Tanner's attorneys had also asked that his conviction be set aside on the basis of newly discovered evidence, including the admission by Noah Covington's children that he appeared to have lied about his whereabouts the night before the killing.

By granting the new trial based solely on the judge's error, the court cleverly avoided bringing up any issue that might bear on the credibility of the one witness whose testimony was the bedrock of the state's case. Tanner's attorneys requested bail for their client as he awaited a new trial. In a brief hearing on the matter in mid-December, Judge Camp ruled that he must remain in jail.

In the meantime, Charlie Rawlings's motion for new trial had come before Judge Camp in mid-November. His attorneys citied nine grounds for reversal, including particularly the statement of Ray Huie. Camp rejected the appeal, kicking the process upward in the legal system.

In Sandersville, Lake Holt was aggressively involved in his new role as the court-appointed administrator of Charlie Rawlings's vast holdings. Despite the conviction of the defendants, the fate and disposition of the insurance policies remained uncertain. In late August following Charlie's conviction, Holt filed suit in Fulton County Superior Court demanding payment, damages, and attorney fees from Prudential Insurance Company for their failure to honor their contractual obligations.

Over the next months, various legal actions regarding the insurance proceeds wended their way through the state and federal court system. In late November, a federal judge in Augusta released $17,000 to Fluker Tarbutton as administrator of his father's estate. A few days later, another federal judge in Atlanta announced that "an amicable agreement" had been reached among the various interested parties in the case, at least so far as the Prudential Insurance Company was concerned. The details of the settlement were "withheld." More than a year later, a final settlement was reached with Southern States Life Insurance Company when the same federal judge ruled that Tarbutton "did not come to his death by accident," effectively voiding the double indemnity provisions of the policies.

Occasional news stories related to the "famous" case dotted the press through the end of 1925, but by early 1926 coverage had moved on to other, more newsworthy topics. In mid-February, the *Sandersville Progress* gave prominent coverage to a sawmill worker who had been sawn in half "from bottom to top" when he was accidentally thrown into the saw apparatus. A week later another sawmill worker died accidentally, this time reported under the front-page headline, "Saw Cuts Off Laborer's Head." It is important to note that a small notice in the paper announced that the 5,000-acre Hancock County farm of the late David Dixon, once one of the most productive and lucrative cotton plantations in the South, had been purchased by an Atlanta real-estate firm. It was to be "cut up into 100 small farms and sold at auction."

On Thursday, March 25, 1926, Jim Tanner's retrial began in the Johnson County Superior Court. The same cast of figures appeared as before, with Judge Earl Camp presiding, Solicitor Fred Kea leading the prosecution, and Willis Evans leading the defense. Tom Hardwick and another of Charlie's attorneys were present, "lending aid wherever [the] interest of C. G. Rawlings appear[ed]." The now-familiar testimony was repeated, with each side aggressively pursuing their positions. Closing arguments were heard, and the case was turned over to the jury near midnight on Saturday. This time, deliberation was brief, with the jury reaching a guilty verdict "soon after deliberation began." Once again, Judge Camp sentenced Tanner to life in prison, and, once again, his attorneys filed an appeal for a new trial.

Shortly after Tanner's reconviction, his son, Ralph Rawlings Tanner, was arrested in Macon on a charge of involuntary manslaughter resulting from an automobile accident in which a pedestrian had been struck and later died. He was quick to assert to a news reporter that he had "no blood ties with C. G. Rawlings, principal defendant with his father in the Tarbutton case." Now, even the once-proud name of Rawlings had become an embarrassment.

In late November 1926, after having had the case for more than a year, the Georgia Supreme Court ruled against granting a new trial to Charlie Rawlings, incidentally rejecting Jim Tanner's appeal at the same time. Rawlings's attorneys had specified fourteen grounds in their appeal. Of these, the justices agreed that thirteen did not warrant reversal of his guilty verdict. On the fourteenth item, the testimony of Ray Huie, the justices were equally divided, with separate written opinions as to how the facts should be interpreted.

In his charge to the jury at the end of Rawlings's trial, Judge Camp had reviewed the subject of confessions, based solely on—according to the appeal—the testimony of Ray Huie, the jailhouse snitch. Under Camp's instructions, the jury would seem to have the option of interpreting the conversation Huie allegedly overheard as a freely given "confession" on the part of Rawlings. Three justices believed this error was of sufficient magnitude to warrant a new trial; three justices did not. In that the court was evenly divided, the ruling of the court of appeals was allowed to stand. A new trial was denied.

On February 17, 1927, exactly two years after the killing on Ring Jaw Bluff, Charlie Rawlings and Jim Tanner were moved to the state penitentiary in Milledgeville to begin serving their life sentences. Despite the setbacks suffered so far, efforts to free Rawlings continued. Even in 1929, more than four years after the initial trials, his case was still of sufficient interest across the state to warrant a mention in the *Atlanta Constitution* that Rawlings's appeal for clemency had been denied by the State Prison Commission, together with that of ten other prisoners, all convicted murderers.

Tom Hardwick, still connected with Charlie Rawlings through friendship and marriage, continued his struggle for Charlie's release. In a letter[1] to his wife dated March 31, 1932, "We argued the C. G. R. matter before Gov. R[ussell] and I think he will parole Charlie." A news item a few days later reported that Hardwick "stated that he was not acting as an attorney, but solely as a former neighbor and friend of Rawlings." The now-convicted murderer was said to be "totally paralyzed" and in "a hopeless physical condition." The State Prison Commission recommended parole. Taking the recommendation under consideration, the governor waited until the Christmas holiday season to grant parole, releasing Charlie on December 24, 1932, after seven years, nine months, and two days in custody. He was seventy-four years old and said to have "only a few months to live."

---

[1] Hardwick 1932.

29

Winners and Losers

One aspect of Chaos Theory (and some branches of religious thought) holds that seemingly random occurrences can be part of a greater train of events that we, as short-lived beings, cannot discern from our limited perspective of time and space. Major trends and sentinel moments are often recognized only in retrospect. Eras are given names, and history is neatly plotted on a time line as if it were indeed following some preordained order. "What if...?" questions are rarely asked, if for no other reason than "It didn't happen that way."

Nearly a century has passed since Gus Tarbutton met his fate on that overcast winter day in February 1925. His death, if a jury's verdict is to be believed, was the ultimate result of an economic disaster known as the Great Recession, which itself was spawned by other diverse events with far-flung roots and origins. If Charlie Rawlings had not achieved economic success in the Golden Age of Georgia's small towns, he would not have faced economic ruin with the crash of the cotton economy and therefore would not have been driven to desperate measures...and the list continues.

Or so the story goes.

Alternatively, perhaps Tarbutton's death was a simple accident, meaning that Rawlings and Tanner were wrongfully convicted, thus taking the subsequent course of history in another direction. Such imponderable questions defy reasonable answers, and one can only discover the facts of history as they seem to exist.

In most of life's great dramas, there are winners and losers, sometimes one and the same. The 1920s was a decade of profound economic, social, and demographic change for Georgia and other states across the Deep South. This observation is clear from the viewpoint of the early twenty-first century, but it scarcely could have been recognized by those leading their daily lives as events unfolded around them. In this light, it may be useful to examine the threads of history as they pertain to the events and actors tied more or less loosely to this complex tale.

In the broadest sense, the biggest losers were Georgia's small towns. While the growth of the state's cities had begun in earnest following the turn of the century, it was only after 1920 that the relative population of rural areas began to stagnate and decline, while urban populations began to increase at an exponential rate. (See Appendix, Figure 5.) Hardest hit were counties whose primary historical economic basis had been the production of cotton. Population losses in these counties were often staggering, with approximately one out of every three persons leaving during the decade in Greene and Hancock counties, for example. In other counties, the immediate exodus was less pronounced. In Burke County, always near the top in cotton production figures, the decade of the 1920s only saw a 5 percent decrease in population, while losses in Johnson, Jefferson, and Washington counties ranged from 6 to 11 percent. The trend that began in the 1920s continued, however, and by 1970—the seeming nadir of population for many of Georgia's rural counties—populations of Burke, Greene, Hancock, Johnson, and Washington counties had shrunk dramatically, with losses ranging from 38 to 51 percent of their 1920 populations.

The exodus of African Americans in the Great Migration certainly contributed to these population declines, but it cannot be cited as the sole or even primary reason in many areas. The 5 percent loss in Burke County in the 1920s came from a population that was 80 percent black. Between 1920 and 1970, however, Georgia's black population declined from approximately 42 percent to 26 percent, due in part both to emigration to other states and the relative increase in the white population. (See Appendix, Figure 6.)

The winners, in terms of population growth, were the state's urban and semi-urban areas, especially those with established mills, factories, and manufacturing facilities. (See Appendix, Figure 7.) The counties in which Macon, Rome, Gainesville, Columbus, and Augusta are located all fulfilled such criteria and grew significantly in the decade following 1920. More important, these and similar cities accounted for essentially all of the subsequent growth in the state's population, while rural area populations declined or grew only minimally.

Agriculture in the state declined in importance after the 1920s, as it did nationally. The collapse of the bubble in cotton prices in 1920, followed immediately by the severest years of the boll weevil's damage, set off a cascade of events that would destroy a large part of the infrastructure that supported the cotton culture. In a self-inductive downward spiral, crop failures led to merchant failures. Merchant failures, the lack of cash in circulation, and the plunge in the value of land led to the shuttering of nearly half of the state's banks. Farm suppliers were battered, ranging from those who sold fertilizer and seeds to the short-line railroads that transported the harvests. Additionally, farming in general was stymied by a shortage of workers as laborers, sharecroppers, and tenant farmers of all stripes faced the inability to make a living, often giving up and moving to other areas and other forms of employment.

By the late 1920s, while it was practically and theoretically possible to achieve cotton yields equal to those of the pre-weevil days, the increased costs and the shortage of manual labor made the crop less attractive. Though tractors were in common use, the general and widespread use of mechanical pickers and similar equipment was decades away. The calls for agricultural diversification, which had gone unheeded for decades, suddenly seemed to make more sense as those who chose to stay on the farm switched to beans, peanuts, orchards, and other less risky crops.

The Ku Klux Klan, which had achieved significant power in the state by mid-decade, declined almost as rapidly as it had risen in its political clout and public support. Battered by its extremes on both a state and national basis, by 1930 the Klan had become a relatively minor fringe element in many areas where it previously held sway. The state legislature, however, remained dominated by rural lawmakers until the latter part of the twentieth century. This was made possible by the so-called County Unit System, established by the legislature in 1917 and in force until declared unconstitutional by the United States Supreme Court in 1963. Under this scheme, the relatively less populous rural counties retained voting power in primary elections disproportionately greater than their population. As Georgia for most of the century was a *de facto* one-party state, a victory in a primary election was usually tantamount to winning the general election. Even after the demise of this method of primary voting, rural lawmakers retained power until late in the century through legislative tenure.

As for the actors in this particular story, Fluker Tarbutton prospered in Wrightsville, at least initially, regaining title to much of his father's land. He eventually moved to town, living in an imposing white frame home on one of the main streets, evidently financially comfortable. Some years later, he had his mother and father exhumed from their burial sites in Sandersville (across the path from the Rawlings plot) and reinterred them in the Wrightsville City Cemetery. Their graves, situated on a small ridge that runs through the burial ground, are now marked by a white marble tomb. Flanked by old cedars, crepe myrtles, and the graves of other citizens whose lives figured prominently in the history of Johnson County, it is the largest monument in the graveyard. Fluker eventually gave up possession of the property containing Ring Jaw Bluff. It was widely reported that he lost it in a poker game.

In Sandersville, Lake Holt prospered as well, or so it seemed. While he continued as president and majority owner of the First National Bank, he had been quietly building a chain of private banks in small agricultural towns across central and south Georgia, all operated under the name Holt Banking Company. Bank closures were common throughout the decade. Holt's strategy was to acquire the assets and deposits of failed banks, reopening them as privately chartered institutions not subject to the usual reporting requirements of state and nationally chartered banks. The First National Bank continued its track record of steady growth and annual dividends as well. In December 1926, more than a year and a half after its closure, Holt purchased the assets of the failed

After Rawlings and Tanner were convicted of the murder of his father, Fluker Tarbutton had his parents' bodies exhumed from the Old City Cemetery in Sandersville and moved to a majestic new marble tomb in the Wrightsville City Cemetery.

Citizens Bank of Sandersville, returning to the few remaining depositors some fifty cents on the dollar.[1]

As Charlie Rawlings sat in jail in Wrightsville, bits and pieces of his prized real estate were sold off. The Santon Hotel, busy and profitable, went in spring 1926. A few months later, the site of the livery stables was sold. These and other financial transactions were arranged by Lake Holt as trustee of Charlie's estate. To one paying close attention to details, the arrangement that granted Holt a $10,000 a year stipend while giving Charlie only $300 a month would appear strange. With his assets so significantly exceeding his liabilities, a $300 monthly allowance would seem to be a mere pittance. As later revealed by a forensic analysis in the courts, Holt's appointment was apparently not an arms-length transaction. Charlie had known Lake Holt for years. They were joint investors in several enterprises, including the Sandersville Railroad and others. In the words of a federal court opinion[2] more than a decade later, "No doubt [Rawlings] had full confidence in Holt, and thought him a desirable person."

While Charlie possessed ample assets, he also had significant debt. Under the circumstances, he had no access to

---

[1] At the time of the Citizens Bank's failure in 1925, there was talk among the shareholders of trying to reopen the bank at a later date. This did not happen. Some three decades later, another Citizens Bank opened in Sandersville, founded by Charlie Rawlings's great-nephew, an inheritor of part of the remaining fortune of Dr. William Rawlings who had died in 1927. The new institution was named the Citizens Bank *of Washington County*. The nephew, a physician, gave up his interest in the bank after somewhat more than a decade, later dying in financial ruin and professional disgrace. The institution went on successfully to become the county's largest locally owned bank.

[2] *First National Bank of Atlanta v. Southern Cotton Oil Company* (1935).

further personal credit, and Holt's appointment as receiver was the result of demands by Charlie's creditors for immediate payment. Holt was—as far as anyone knew—a wealthy businessman and an accomplished banker with access to funding to cover Charlie's immediate debts. The plan— apparently worked out with Charlie's input and approval— was for Holt to issue some $200,000 in short-term notes to satisfy the creditors who had brought suit, then use the income from farming operations and limited sales of assets to retire the notes. "It is clear that [Charlie] expected to get his property back at the end of two years at most." Charlie's son Fred, apparently out of the car business in Atlanta,[3] was employed by Holt to assist him in the management of the numerous farms and businesses.

For several years, matters seemed to run smoothly. The miserable economy continued, making rapid payoff of Charlie's debts impossible, or so said Lake Holt, who remained in touch with the prisoner. "Practically every act was fully known and approved by Mr. Rawlings and his son, W. F. Rawlings," Holt would later state to the local paper.[4] This seemed not to hinder the expansion of the Holt Banking Company, which in late February 1929 opened a branch in Alma, Georgia, the twelfth in addition to those in Avera, Bartow, Ludowici, Cobbtown, Harrison, Warthen, Davisboro, Register, Mansfield, Midville, and Rocky Branch.

---

[3] Fred had been in business with Holt's son, Ben, but the partnership appears to have been dissolved sometime in mid-1925. Ben moved back to Sandersville and died at age 36 in August of that year after what was said to be a brief illness. No clear cause of death is given on the death certificate (Georgia's Virtual Vault, http://cdm.sos.state.ga.us). The local newspaper said he died of "either apoplexy or congestion."

[4] *Sandersville Progress*, 12 August 1925.

Approximately two weeks later, Charlie's daughter filed suit against Lake Holt for the mismanagement of her father's estate. Holt responded by calling the allegations in the suit "absolutely untrue," claiming that a closer analysis would reveal "a faithful execution of the trust."[5] He urged the public to withhold judgment until the truth could be revealed in court.

Within days, the twelve banks of the Holt Banking Company closed without warning. Floy Holt, another of Holt's sons employed as vice president of the First National Bank, announced confidently, "None of the depositors will lose a penny," adding that they hoped to reopen in ten days.[6] The following day, depositors began a run on the First National Bank in Sandersville, rapidly depleting it of cash on hand. The next day, that bank, too—the flagship of the empire—failed to open. Within days, warrants were issued for the arrest of Lake Holt and Floy Holt, charging embezzlement at the Alma and Ludowici branches of Holt Banking Company. Lake Holt issued a statement alleging, "I am absolutely solvent and have sufficient funds to pay all depositors and creditors in full." He denied the misappropriation of funds and urged his creditors "to cooperate with me."[7]

An avalanche of lawsuits followed in both state and federal courts, not only from Holt's many creditors but also from Charlie Rawlings's children. The *Sandersville Progress*, evidently still having faith in Holt's denial of culpability, referred to the bank closings as the result of "an unfortunate chain of events," noting he had received many letters and personal assurances from his supporters who trusted his

---

[5] Ibid., 13 March 1929.

[6] *Atlanta Constitution*, 14 March 1929.

[7] Ibid., 19 March 1929.

"integrity and honesty." The paper blamed the depositors of Holt's banks for their failure, stating "such withdrawals of deposits will break any bank in the United States if kept up long enough." Holt was described as "a man of unblemished character [who] enjoys the confidence and esteem of all who know him."[8]

The First National Bank was taken over by the comptroller of the currency. Initial reports—as recounted by the *Progress*—revealed that assets "greatly exceed" liabilities, offering some hope to the bank's depositors. The suits against Holt were consolidated in federal court with a trial scheduled for late summer. Under pressure from many fronts, Holt finally admitted that he had no resources to pay his creditors. The court refused to remove him as the trustee for the Rawlings estate but did enjoin him from disposing of any assets.

As the summer months passed, it became evident that the "assets" of the First National Bank, the Holt Banking Company, and Lake Holt personally were—for the most part—promissory notes and other uncollectible intangibles. His liabilities, on the other hand, totaled $737,152.15, much of it owed to the depositors and other creditors of his failed banks.

With Holt now adjudged bankrupt, the federal judge hearing his case removed him as trustee of the Rawlings estate, appointing instead I. W. Arnold, cashier of the failed First National Bank and one of Holt's close associates. After taking inventory of the remaining assets in the estate, he issued a year-end report to the judge stating that many were "practically worthless." Arnold resigned as trustee shortly thereafter.

During summer and fall 1929, and especially following the testimony given at Holt's bankruptcy proceedings, his role

---

[8] 3 April 1929.

in the failure of the First National Bank was investigated by agents of the Justice Department. In January 1930, Newman Wood and H. M Franklin, two local businessmen from Washington County, were appointed by the court to take over as receivers of the Rawlings estate. They were specifically charged with the Herculean task of providing a new inventory of what remained in the estate and what had happened to it under Holt's tenure as trustee. Wood, a meticulous and compulsive diarist, kept an exquisitely detailed record of the new trustees' every action over the next year.[9] The pair immediately discovered widespread evidence of fiduciary mismanagement and outright fraud by Holt, his son, and various business associates. Based on this and other evidence uncovered at the bankruptcy hearings, Lake Holt, Floy Holt, I. W. Arnold (the second Rawlings estate trustee), and one other bank officer were indicted in late 1930 on more than seventy counts of embezzlement, fraud, misapplication of funds and false reporting involving the failure of the First National Bank, and the mismanagement of the estate of Charles G. Rawlings.

The trial of Lake and Floy Holt took place in Macon in May 1931. In a strange twist of fate, it was in large part the Rawlings estate that gave the Holts the ability to hide their financial misdeeds, and this formed the basis of the government's case. The notes originally created to raise funds to pay the estate's indebtedness were "manipulated [in] many of their fraudulent schemes," according to the testimony of the FBI agent who acted as lead investigator in the case. Using a series of "sham corporations," unsecured promissory notes, and off-the-books accounting, the Holts managed to give the appearance of a financially healthy bank, when in fact it had been looted for their personal gain. They were convicted on

---

[9] Wood n.d.

multiple counts. In their sentencing, the judge noted that their crimes made it possible for him to impose "a sentence of from seventy-five to one hundred years," but he gave them each eighteen months based on Lake Holt's formerly "influential" life. No mention was made of the damage done to Charlie Rawlings, then completing his sixth year of incarceration. The lawsuits arising from Holt's mismanagement of Charlie's estate continued, with the last case settled in 1935.

By the end of the decade, nine of the eleven banks that were in business in Washington County at its start had failed or otherwise ceased business. Farming remained a financially risky endeavor. As events unfolded, the financial future of the county appeared to be hidden beneath its soil. The Middle Georgia Oil & Gas Company had failed to find the "vast pool of oil," but their drilling had revealed the existence of equally vast beds of high-quality clays. The clay-mining industry, which had taken hold in neighboring Wilkinson County, began to shift toward Washington County. Bauxite mining, once touted as the route to riches, faltered after only a few years, but kaolin was destined by the end of the century to become a multi-billion-dollar industry, creating many millionaires from otherwise struggling landowners who had so long eked out a living from farming.

At the time of his arrest, Charlie Rawlings had been the president of the Sandersville Railroad. In spring 1927, Lake Holt sold Rawlings's remaining interest[10] in the line (some 80

---

[10] The Sandersville Railroad was founded in the early 1890s. According to an 1894 notice of a stockholders' meeting found in family documents, there were at the time at least 32 initial shareholders owning a total of 100 shares of stock. Interestingly, one of them was T. J. Elder, a well-respected African-American educator from Sandersville. In the three-plus decades that followed, the stock

shares out of a total of 200) to Ben Tarbutton, first cousin to both Charlie and the now-deceased Gus Tarbutton. Ben had been the manager of the enterprise since 1915 and had acquired stock from other shareholders. Now owning the majority of the railroad's shares, he assumed his cousin's former role as president.

Short-line railroads across the state were at perilous risk of failure. Charles Molony, the president of the Wrightsville & Tennille and three other short lines, leapt to his death from the fourth floor of a Savannah hotel in August 1930. He had been connected with railroads for forty-one of his sixty years and was said to be suffering from "a serious nervous breakdown." Ben Tarbutton, a savvy businessman, built spur lines to serve the growing kaolin mining industry, eventually turning the

---

had split, yielding 200 shares, and had been sold and resold many times on a private basis. On April 20, 1927, under the headline "Railroad Stock Changes Hands," the *Sandersville Progress* reported that 80 shares had sold to Ben Tarbutton for $12,000. On the assumption that this represented 40 percent of the line's ownership, the worth of the entire railroad would appear to be only $30,000, a minuscule figure even by current standards of the day. The news item specifically noted that the railroad was in good shape financially, stating, "This is one of the highest dividend paying short lines in the country and enjoys a very large business." The interested reader will recall that several years earlier Charlie had apparently given 80 additional shares to his brother, Ben Rawlings, in settlement of their father's estate. Whether or not these shares were actually transferred cannot be documented, as the railroad was (and remains) a closely held corporation. On the assumption that they were, Charlie had apparently owned at least 80 percent of the shares at one time. The bargain price for the shares in 1927 seems strange, to say the least. The sale occurred shortly after Charlie's transfer to prison but more than two years before Lake Holt's criminal mismanagement of the Rawlings estate was revealed.

few miles of rail into a lucrative enterprise while many other of the state's short-line railroads failed in the 1920s and 1930s.

While the kaolin industry breathed some life into the economy of Washington County, the decline of agriculture took its toll over the coming decades. In Sandersville, the gins ceased operation, and the rows of warehouses that once were packed with cotton fell into disrepair and were eventually torn down. Charlie Rawlings's once-magnificent house on the corner of Church and Harris streets suffered the indignity of having a filling station built in its expansive yard, cheek-on-jowl next to its balustraded porch. With its paint peeling but its magnolias still providing shade, the home became a boarding house known as the Magnolia Inn, the etched initials of "CGR" remaining on the glass of the grand front door to mock its disgraced owner. A late 1930s guide[11] to Georgia prepared by the Writers' Program of the Works Progress Administration awarded Sandersville a dismissive single-sentence description as "pleasantly old-fashioned in its architecture and restful shady streets."

Tennille, the bustling town whose fortunes were founded on its status as a railroad nexus, faded with the death of short-line railroads. Choate's houses still dot its streets, a century or more old now, but its central market area has become a graveyard of abandoned and decaying buildings.

Wrightsville, whose economy was almost totally dependent on agriculture, suffered as well, slipping into a gradual decline that has continued to the present day. The Ku Klux Klan remained strong there for a number of years after its support waned elsewhere in the state. Jim Johnson, the negro who had placed a curse on the courthouse clock just before his death by lynching in 1922, finally had his day. In February

---

[11] Georgia Board of Education 1940.

1938, the thousand-pound weight that powered the clock gave way and crashed through the second floor courtroom and to the ground floor below, wreaking extensive damage in its path. Old-timers said the dead man was having his revenge.

Jim Tanner was finally released from prison some months after Charlie Rawlings gained his freedom. His health had declined and—according to family members—he was sent home to die. He succumbed to apparent tuberculosis shortly after his release and was buried in the graveyard of a country church near Sandersville.

Despite the reports of his near-terminal condition, Charlie Rawlings did well after his release from prison in December 1932. He moved into an old farmhouse on the western edge of town, living independently and dividing his time between there and the plantation home of his late brother, now occupied by his niece. From the front porch of his new home, he could see the city cemetery and, in the distance, fields of cotton stretching toward the western horizon, a vista of both his future and his past. He was occasionally seen hanging out on the benches of the City Square with other old men whose productive lives were behind them. In those days, many smoked Bull Durham tobacco, rolling their own cigarettes from a drawstring pouch sealed with a folding metal clip about the size of a dime. The streets were littered with these discarded clips, appearing to the casual observer as lost coins in the gutter. One observer, a relative of both Charlie Rawlings and Gus Tarbutton, sadly recalls Charlie as a bent old man with a cane poking at the discarded clips in hopes of finding a bit of change.

Charlie Rawlings was said to have died quietly in his sleep on November 15, 1938, never having recovered any of his lost fortune. His obituary was carried in a number of newspapers, describing him as "once one of the most prosperous businessmen of this section," but having lost heavily "when the boll weevil first made its appearance in Washington County." No mention was made of the Tarbutton affair, and his death certificate listed his occupation simply as "farmer." He was buried in the family plot in Sandersville's Old City Cemetery, his final resting place marked only with an anonymous concrete slab. No photographs of him are known to exist.

30

Thoughts

History is often written by the winners, but even then it is rarely remembered with accuracy as the sharp details of the persons, places, and events that played a role are worn smooth by the flow of time. To most of modern America, the period following World War I has become known as the Roaring Twenties, a period of urbanity and economic growth. This era is said to have ended abruptly with the Wall Street Crash of 1929, leading to the Great Depression that lasted until the country's entry into World War II. The history of the rural South, however, followed a different path, now almost faded to obscurity in the brighter light of the larger course of American history. For Georgia, a state whose population was relatively rural and dependant on agriculture, the Great Depression began not with the 1929 collapse of the stock market, but in January 1920 with the collapse of the cotton economy. While much of the rest of the nation prospered, the small market towns that had characterized the state for more than a century began a spiraling decline from which most would not recover.

History is often also recorded in terms of events and outcomes, glossing over the effect on individual lives. Wars are won or lost, with innocent deaths taking the ubiquitous name of "collateral damage." Economies wax and wane, described in retrospect as expansions or depressions, rarely remembering those who prospered or failed in the process. Charlie Rawlings, Gus Tarbutton, Jim Tanner, Lake Holt, and others of this tale were men of their time, variously victors or victims or both, based on their individual circumstances and on forces beyond their control. Through their recorded roles in this saga, however, they provide a window on history's events as they swirled through the lives of ordinary folk.

I have no idea whether or not Charlie Rawlings and Jim Tanner were guilty of the murder of Gus Tarbutton. History's record has adjudged them as such, and nothing can change that. The facts and details, viewed from nearly a century later, might suggest that the validity of their convictions and sentences should be viewed with suspicion. Charlie Rawlings had his faults. There is ample evidence of his immorality and at least suggestive evidence of his indifference to the rule of law when it stood in the way of his personal goals and needs. Perhaps he was no different from many of his era, when America was a different place and rules were made to be broken. Or perhaps he was someone who finally met his deserved fate, and his conviction—right or wrong—was delivered not so much because of what he may or may not have done but because of what everyone knew he was capable of doing. Jim Tanner, whether complicit in a murder conspiracy or not, was clearly a victim of circumstance.

There are some, particularly in the Rawlings and Tanner families, who firmly believe that the convictions of their relatives were the result of a conspiracy, the product of "bought testimony," to echo Tom Hardwick's words. They cite others who stood to gain financially by Charlie's fall or wanted to get retribution for wrongs he had done them over the years. Other family members are not so sure, having said he was capable of anything, including murder, in his desperate attempt to avoid financial failure. One attorney who took an interest in the case saw judicial malfeasance, stating, "In those days, it was cheaper for the insurance companies to buy a few judges than pay a huge settlement." There is no objective evidence for this. In the end, both Rawlings and Tanner died with the stigma of murder forever staining their names.

Appendix

Figure 1

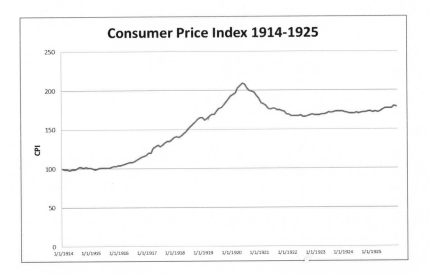

The 1916 to 1920 time frame represented the single greatest period of sustained inflation in United States history from the founding of the Republic to the present day. The purchasing power of the dollar was roughly halved in a five-year period. (Source: US Department of Labor Bureau of Labor Statistics, http://www.bls.gov/cpi/tables.htm)

Figure 2

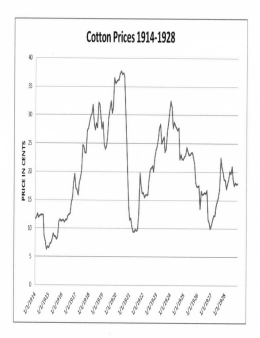

The trading price of cotton in then-current dollars increased more than five times by 1920 compared to its low point in late 1914. These figures are uncorrected for inflation. (Source: Data graph derived from USDA *Yearbook of Agriculture* statistics)

Figure 3

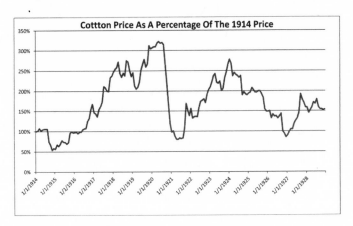

The trading price of cotton in then-current dollars increased more than five times by 1920 compared to its low point in late 1914. These figures are uncorrected for inflation. (Source: Data graph derived from USDA *Yearbook of Agriculture* statistics.)

Figure 4

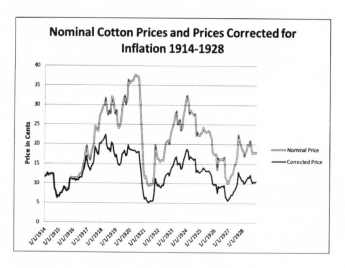

While cotton prices rose dramatically between 1916 and 1920, inflation did also. The "Nominal Price" shown in the graph reflects the current trading value of cotton in this time frame. The "Corrected Price" reflects the value of cotton corrected by the Consumer Price Index. This adjustment of value is a crude measurement at best, but it clearly indicates that when cotton peaked near forty cents in 1920, the purchasing power of the inflated dollar was roughly half of what it had been some four to five years earlier. (Source: Data graphs derived from USDA *Yearbook of Agriculture* statistics and US Department of Labor Bureau of Labor Statistics CPI data)

Figure 5

TREND IN TOTAL POPULATION

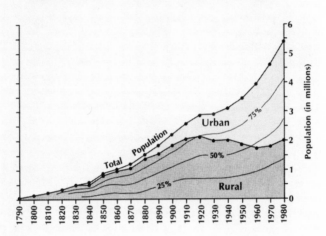

The vast majority of population growth in Georgia took place in rural areas (i.e., towns and villages with a population of less than 2,500 persons) up until the decade of the 1920s. After this, rural grow stagnated and declined while urban areas grew rapidly. (From *The Atlas of Georgia*. Reproduced with permission.)

Figure 6

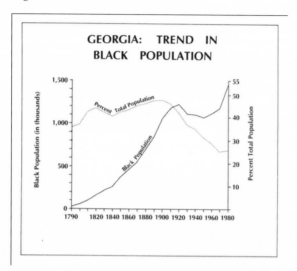

Georgia's African-American population grew rapidly with the cotton-based economy, peaking as a percentage of the total population in the late nineteenth century and in absolute numbers in 1920. Starting in the decade of the 1920s, both figures decreased, stabilizing and increasing only in the latter quarter of the twentieth century. (From *The Atlas of Georgia*. Reproduced with permission.)

Figure 7

A Comparison of Population Changes in Selected Rural vs. Urban Georgia Counties Following the Great Recession of 1920

Georgia County (County Seat)	Population Change 1920-1930	Population Change 1920-1970	Population Change 1920-2010
Burke (Waynesboro)	-5%	-41%	-24%
Greene (Greensboro)	-34%	-46%	-16%
Hancock (Sparta)	-29%	-51%	-51%
Jefferson (Louisville)	-8%	-24%	-25%
Johnson (Wrightsville)	-6%	-43%	-26%
Washington (Sandersville)	-11%	-38%	-25%

Rural Counties With A Historical Primary Agricultural Base

Georgia County (County Seat)	Population Change 1920-1930	Population Change 1920-1970	Population Change 1920-2010
Bibb (Macon)	+ 8%	+101%	+218%
Floyd (Rome)	+22%	+85%	+242%
Hall (Gainesville)	+13%	+221%	+670%
Muscogee (Columbus)	+30%	+379%	+430%
Richmond (Augusta)	+15%	+255%	+315%

Urban and Semi-Urban Counties With Large Dependence on Mills and Manufacturing

Chapter Notes

Occasionally, there are other bits of information, perspective, and explanation that do not warrant footnotes but seem to require more than a simple reference citation. I present these here for the interested reader.

Chapter 6: The accounts of the shootings of Fred Rawlings and Richard Roughton were reported in detail in contemporary issues of the *Sandersville Herald & Georgian* and the *Middle Georgia Progress*. Additional information on the details of the 1890 lawsuit was drawn from a Roughton family genealogy website (http://roughton-maas. com/sandersville_ shootout.htm) and from public records of the Georgia Supreme Court.

Chapter 7: A strange incident is told about Gus Tarbutton. In January 1898, an infant was left on the porch of an older couple who lived between Wrightsville and Tennille, near the Johnson-Wash-ington County line. Attached was a note saying the baby girl had been born three weeks earlier. In later years, she wrote that her adoptive parents said they knew nothing of her true heritage, only that the person who left her there was named Gus Tarbutton.[1] He would have been twenty-two years of age at the time.

The details of the account of the Tyre murder and the court proceedings that followed were drawn from contemporary issues of the *Wrightsville Chronicle*, the *Dublin Courier-Dispatch*, and the *Sander-sville Herald*.

The original of the 1907 survey plat that defined the new Laurens-Johnson county borders is in the Georgia Archives in Morrow, Georgia. At the time, surveying methods were quite crude as compared to the present day, and significant variations between old and new surveys of the same area were not uncommon. The line in question was measured by the surveyor Robert as 28,763 feet in length. Neither end has a clearly defined point, and points that de-mark the line are designated on the plat with such terms as "beech," "oak," "pine," "marked tree," and the like, none of which have exact locations given. In the forty-nine years between the initial and repeat surveys, there were no significant technological changes that would have improved the precision of the later survey. It is reasonable to say that the accuracy of this survey can be assumed to be the same as the earlier one, but for the purposes of those requesting it, the results were more favorable. The actual site of Tyre's killing is

---

[1] Dukes 1961.

unknown. From a current perspective, it appears impossible to determine in which county the murder actually took place.

Chapter 17: Viewed from a historical perspective, there appears to be little doubt that the "Beach oil field" in western Washington County and the Middle Georgia Oil & Gas Company that promoted it were little more than scams designed to milk the gullible public of hard-earned money. The slickly written ads and the parade of "oil men" alleged to be from the petroleum-producing states of the West should have, if nothing else, aroused suspicions. More important, in the intervening decades the clay beds discovered incidentally in the drilling process have been extensively mined with no further evidence of a "vast pool of oil beneath."

One of the first serious attempts to find oil in Georgia was a well drilled in neighboring Jefferson County in 1905 by Captain A. F. Lucas, the same man who first discovered oil in the famed Spindletop Field near Beaumont, Texas, in 1901.[2] The well was abandoned after reaching a depth of approximately 500 feet with no evidence of oil or gas. Two years later, the Georgia Petroleum Oil Company took over the well and drilled to 1,143 feet before striking rock and giving up.

Early wildcatters had little or no geologic evidence to suggest the presence of oil fields beneath the earth. Exploration was based on "shows" of petroleum-like substances or natural gas, both of which could have been due to decaying organic matter. Interestingly, in the latter third of the twentieth century a serious attempt was made to find oil in Washington County.[3] Based in some part on the "shows" but also on geologic structures that might be associated with the presence of trapped oil and/or gas, large areas of oil leases were assembled and four exploratory wells were sunk. In 1978, a 4,200-foot-deep well was drilled on the Taylor farm near Davisboro in the eastern part of the county. Some natural gas was found, but nothing remotely near commercial quantities. The well was logged and capped. In 1980, three additional wells were drilled within a few miles of the Taylor well. A 5,600-foot well came up dry. A 3,800-foot well was abandoned when no oil had been found and the drill bit broke. Finally, a deep well was sunk to a depth of nearly10,000 feet before being abandoned. There is no current evidence that oil and gas exists or has ever existed in the earth of Washington County.

Chapter 18: The Klan was a major force in Georgia life and politics for a fairly brief period between about 1920 and 1925, when, wounded by its own

---

[2] S. W. McCallie 1919.

[3] Taylor 2011.

corruption and violence, it faded rapidly from the state and national scene. The brief history of the Klan given here is drawn from several sources. The following works represent an excellent overview with much detail:

Chalmers, David M. *Hooded Americanism: The History of the Ku Klux Klan.* Durham: Duke University Press, 1987.
Horn, Stanley F. *Invisible Empire: The Story of the Ku Klux Klan 1866–1871.* Montclair NJ: Patterson Smith Publishing Corporation, 1969.
Jackson, Kenneth T. *The Ku Klux Klan in the City 1915–1930.* New York: Oxford University Press, 1967.
MacLean, Nancy. *Behind the Mask of Chivalry.* New York: Oxford University Press, 1994.
Wade, Wyn C. *The Fiery Cross.* New York: Oxford University Press, 1987.

A fascinating bit of contemporary insight can be gained from reading the United States House of Representatives Hearing on "The Ku Klux Klan" held by the Committee on Rules in October 1921. Much of the transcript consists of the testimony of William J. Simmons and gives his perspective on the early days of the Klan. Several appendices and exhibits document Klan finances and rituals. Published versions of this work are available at no charge in electronic form, the most convenient source being Google Books.

Some of the "local" lore, including the details of Charlie Rawlings's castration, is derived from personal family history and confirmed through others who were aware of the incident. The details are all quite consistent, the only question being which of his many sins Charlie was punished for.

The Klan nominally remained entrenched in Johnson County well past the 1930s. During that decade, they were said to have castrated another man, a Jewish physician who was accused of marital infidelity. It is interesting to note that the *World Book Encyclopedia* of the early 1960s illustrated its entry for "Ku Klux Klan" with a photo of a group of Klansmen in full regalia standing in a circle around a burning cross and the American flag. The photo was taken on the grounds of the Johnson County courthouse in spring 1948.

Chapter 25: Unless otherwise noted, all quotes are taken directly from the trial transcript. I have occasionally made minor changes in spelling and punctuation for clarity, but otherwise have reproduced the sometimes confusing syntax and conjugation.

Author's Note and Acknowledgments

On a practical basis, reconstructing the series of events detailed in this book presented some difficulties. Almost no one is living with adult firsthand knowledge of the 1890s through 1925. To tell the story, I have relied on newspaper accounts and on interviews with relatives, business associates, acquaintances, and friends of the persons involved as well as those with a working knowledge of the cotton economy and the rural South.

The families of both C. G. Rawlings and Jim Tanner have long held reservations about their relatives' guilt in the death of Gus Tarbutton. Clearly, there were those who—for whatever reason—felt otherwise. In 1947, Tanner's daughter set out to try to clear her father's name. She encountered missing court records and received "threats of physical danger." In 1978, a student at Georgia College in Milledgeville chose the 1906 murders and the subsequent 1925 death of Gus Tarbutton as a topic for her Master's thesis. She, too, received threats and intimidation. In consideration of "the very difficult (if not dangerous) circumstances," she was advised by her professor to abandon her inquiries. In my research for this work in 2009 through 2011, I found no such overt resistance, but by then most who would not want events of the past revisited had likely passed into eternity. Numerous individuals have provided willing and eager assistance in my research, though some did so on a private basis.

While some of the material in this book may be contro-versial, I have done my best to winnow out the rumors, innu-endo, and unsubstantiated opinions that often accompanied the gathering of data. I have tried to identify clearly any conclusions or conjectures made from the author's perspective.

There are many people without whose assistance, knowl-edge, and advice this work would have not been possible. Some have asked to remain anonymous, and I will respect their requests. First and foremost, I must thank my wife, the former Elizabeth Dunwody of Macon, for her support and forbearance in allowing me the time to pursue this project. Donald Smith of Wrightsville has done much to preserve the history of Johnson County and was kind enough to provide the transcript of Jim Tanner's 1925 trial in addition to access to historical news-papers from Johnson County. He and Ron Taylor also took me on a boat trip up the Oconee River to see Ring Jaw Bluff for myself. Dan Roper, publisher of *Georgia Backroads* magazine, offered encouragement and feedback, both for the initial magazine article and for this work. My cousin and friend Strick Newsom gave able assistance with the complex family relationships that exist in small towns, as did others. Scott

Thompson first brought to my attention the 1906 killings and showed interest in this project as it progressed. James Frances and David Brooker of the current Citizens Bank of Washington County helped me sort through two decades of financial reports on the Citizens Bank of Sandersville, giving me insight on how and why it failed. Loretta Cato and Kayla Jackson, along with other volunteer members of Washington County Historical Society, provided valuable input and helped me follow up on historical leads. My assistant Brandi Taylor and my office nurse Jessica Heldreth were immensely helpful, attending to many details that I would otherwise be respon-sible for, thus freeing me to do research and write. Jolene Lindsey assisted in preparation of the graphs and tables displayed in the Appendix. Judge Walter C. McMillan provided assistance in tracking down legal cases. Bob Wynne, Mary Eleanor Wickersham, Amanda Polglase, Clyde Wright, Anne Brooker, Carol Gray, Benjie Tarbutton, and others reviewed drafts of my writing and provided valuable feedback. Gene Veal, Herschel Lovett, Joe Rowland, Isabel Snyder, Leon Lovett, Lewis West, Marsha Moore, Merlene Thompson, Nelda Erwin, Phil Boatright, Ervin Cordry, Ray Taylor, Rebbie Wright, Robert F. Smith, Sam Goodrich, W. A. Phillips, and others who wished to remain anonymous provided insight and history in oral interviews. The staff of the probate judge of Washington County generously put up with weeks of allowing me to read hundreds of old newspapers from the late nineteenth and early twentieth centuries. Other newspapers were made available through the microfilm collection of the University of Georgia Library in Athens. I appreciate the support and assistance provided by Marc Jolley, Marsha Luttrell, and others at Mercer University Press. Finally, I must—as always—thank my muse, the ineffable Laura Ashley, without whose inspiration life would be most dull.

I hope the reader finds this work both interesting and educational. I welcome comments and feedback via mail at Post Office Box 737, Sandersville, Georgia, 31082, or email at rawlings@pascuamanagment.com. Feel free to visit my website at www.williamrawlings.com for additional information on my other writings and news of current interest.

Sources and Context

The vast majority of the "local" events recounted in this work are drawn from contemporary newspapers, most frequently the *Sandersville Progress* (and its predecessors, the *Georgian* and *Herald*) and the *Wrightsville Headlight*. These were—and are—typical small-town weeklies, the main sources of local news and gossip for rural communities for decades prior to the advent of electronic communications. As seemed to be the standard of the day, reporting was often detailed and opinionated, with the most trivial items worthy of coverage. Local papers also published (often without attribution) news and stories of interest from other sources, including magazines, newspapers, and, later, news wire services. Some items are from the state's dailies (e.g., the *Atlanta Constitution* or the *Augusta Chronicle*), but I have tried to make such references clear in the text.

Generally speaking, I have not provided individual footnotes for quotes from local newspapers, but the context should be obvious to the reader, even when referring to regional or national events. For other sources, I have provided references as appropriate. In reproducing quotes, I have tried to maintain the often awkward syntax, punctuation, and capitalization but have occasionally made corrections of typos and misspellings, noting these as necessary.

As the economy of cotton is one of the central themes of this book, I make frequent mention of the price of cotton. Cotton, like many farm products, is a widely traded commodity, and its price varies from moment to moment and place to place. There is considerable mark-up in the price as the raw fiber moves from field to gin to warehouse to the transportation system and finally to the mill. There is variability based on the quality of the cotton and other factors. The prices I cite are taken from United States Department of Agriculture publications (generally *Yearbooks of Agriculture*) and reflect the average prices paid to the farmer for sales of baled cotton.

In any literary work having to do with the American South, the subject of race is always a sensitive issue, and per-haps a bit of explanation is appropriate. Generally speaking, the reader will note that among other designations I commonly use the term "negro" (non-capitalized) to refer to African Americans. This choice of words was made for contextual rea-sons. In reading thousands of pages of contemporary literature in preparing this work, overwhelmingly the most common term used to refer to persons of color was "negro." Commonly, but less frequently, the term "colored" would be used, especially in government publications (e.g., the US Census) or when the writer was feeling benevolent. The term "black" was rarely used, and the term "darky" (or "darkie") seemed to be limited to conversational speech. Only once did I come across "Afro American." This was in a publication from Booker T. Washington's Tuskegee Institute. The current popular appellation "African American" dates from the 1980s and was not in use in the time frame covered by this book.

Contemporary Newspapers Referenced
    Atlanta Georgian
    Atlanta Constitution
    Augusta Chronicle
    Dublin Courier-Dispatch
    Macon News
    Macon Telegraph
    Middle Georgia Progress
    Sandersville Progress
    Sandersville Herald
    Sandersville Georgian
    Sandersville Herald & Georgian
    Savannah Morning News
    Savannah Press
    Soperton News
    Wrightsville Chronicle
    Wrightsville Headlight

Other References and Sources

Alston, L. G., W. Grove, and D. C. Wheelock. "Structural Causes of Rural Bank Failures in the Twenties." *The Cliometric Society*. 1990.

Anonymous. Letter to Attorney General. Sandersville GA. 3 May 1921.

Averitt, Jack N. *Families of Southeastern Georgia*. Baltimore: Genealogical Publishing Company, 2007.

Brooks et al. v. Rawlings (1912). 138 Ga. 310;75 S.E. 157.

Brooks et al. v. Rawlings (1921). 152 Ga. 394; 110 S.E. 159.

Cash, W. J. *The Mind of the South*. New York: A. A. Knopf, 1941.

Chalmers, David M. *Hooded Americanism: The History of the Ku Klux Klan*. Durham: Duke University Press, 1987.

Coleman, Kenneth. *A History of Georgia*. Athens: University of Georgia Press, 1991.

Dattel, Gene. *Cotton and Race in the Making of America*. Chicago: Ivan R. Dee, 2009.

Dukes, Willie K. "The Story of the Life of Willie Hubert Killlingwoth Bridges Dukes." Autobiography. No publisher. 1961.

Eaton, Clement. *The Growth of Southern Civilization*. New York: Harper & Brothers, 1961.

First National Bank of Atlanta v. Southern Cotton Oil Company. 78 F.2d 339 (1935) (US Fifth Circuit Court of Appeals, 7 June 1935).

Georgia Board of Education. *Georgia: A Guide to Its Towns and Countryside*. Athens: University of Georgia Press, 1940.

Gordy, Berry. Sr. *Movin' Up*. New York: Harper & Row, 1979.

Haney, P. B., W. J. Lewis, W. R. Lambert. *Cotton Production and the Boll Weevil in Georgia*. The Georgia Agricultural Experiment Stations, 1996.

Hardwick, Thomas W. Letter to Maude Hardwick. 31 March 1932.

Harris, Joel C. *Life of Henry W. Grady*. New York: Cassell Publishng Company, 1890.

Horn, Stanley F. *Invisible Empire: The Story of the Ku Klux Klan 1866–1871*. Montclair NJ: Patterson Smith Publishing Corporation, 1969.

Hux, Roger K. "The Ku Klux Klan in Macon, 1915–1925." *The Georgia Historical Quarterly* (1978): 155–68.

Institute of Community and Area Development. *The Atlas of Georgia*. Athens: Univeristy of Georgia, 1986.

Jackson, Kenneth T. *The Ku Klux Klan in the City 1915–1930*. New York: Oxford University Press, 1967.

Jordan, Mary Alice. *A History of Washington County Georgia 1784–1989*. Roswell GA: W. H. Wolfe Associates, 1989.

Knight, Lucian Lamar. *A Standard History of Georgia and Georgians*. Chicago: Lewis Publishing Company, 1917.

Lang, W.G. et al. *Bauxite and Kaolin Deposits of the Irwinton Distict Georgai*. Washington: US Government Printing Office, 1965.

MacLean, Nancy. *Behind the Mask of Chivalry*. New York: Oxford University Press, 1994.

McCallie, S. W., J. P. D. Hull, L. P. Teas. *A Preliminary Report on the Oil Prospect near Scotland, Telfair County, Georgia*. Atlanta: Index Printing Company, 1919.

National Cotton Producers Association. www.cottonseedoiltour.com.

Porcher, Richard D., and Sarah Fick. *The Story of Sea Island Cotton*. Layton UT: Wyrick & Company, 2005.

Range, Willard. *A Century of Georgia Agriculture*. Athens: University of Georgia Press, 1954.

Rawlings v. Brown (1914). 15 Ga. App. 162, S.E. 803.

Rawlings v. State (1926). 163 Ga. 406, 136 S.E. 448

Rawlings, William. "The Genius of Georgia Architect Charles E. Choate." *Georgia Backroads*. Winter 2009.

Scherer, James A. B. *Cotton as a World Power*. New York: Frederick A. Stokes Co., 1916.

Shivers, Forest. *The Land Between: A History of Hancock County to 1940*. Spartanburg: The Reprint Company, 1990.

Smiley, Gene. "The US Economy in the 1920s." *Eh.net*. 1 February 2010. http://eh.net/encyclopedia/article/smiley.1920s.final (accessed May 2011).

Smith, Richard W. *Sedimentary Kaolins of the Coastal Plain of Georgia*. Atlanta: Stein Printing Company, 1929.

South Carolina Boll Weevil Commission. *Boll Weevil*. Washington: US Government Printing Office, 1921. Revised edition.

Stowe, Harriet Beecher. "Our Florida Plantation." *The Atlantic*. May 1879.

Suttler, Bernard. *Makers of America: Georgia Edition*. Atlanta: A. B. Caldwell, 1912.

Taylor, Ray. Interview by William Rawlings. 18 August 2011.

United States Census. 1860, 1910, and 1920.

United States Department of Agriculture. "The Mexican Cotton-Boll Weevil." 1901.

———. *Yearbook of Agriculture*. 1910, 1911, 1920.

United States Department of Labor. *Consumer Price Index*. http://www.bls.gov/cpi/tables.htm.

Vernon, J. R. "The 1920–21 Deflation: The Role of Aggregate Supply." *Economic Inquiry*. 1991.

Wood, J. Hines. Letter to William Rawlings. 17 August 1971.

Wood, Newman. "Diary for 1930." In the private collection of William Rawlings, Jr.

Woodward, C. Vann. *Tom Watson: Agrarian Rebel*. New York: Oxford University Press, 1963.

World Book Encyclopedia. Field Enterprises Educational Corporation, 1963.

Yaffa, Stephen. *Cotton: The Biography of a Revolutionay Fiber*. New York: Penguin Books, 2005.

Index

Index

Roughton, Lavinia Rawlings, 41, 46
Roughton, Richard, 41, 43
rural economy post-Civil War, 30
Sandersville: description of, 1, 8, 10, 58-60, 91, 250; population in 1903, 58; population in 1916, 91
Sandersville Railroad, 37, 59, 79, 82, 85,103, 107, 124, 146, 148, 158-59, 213, 243, 248-250
sawmills, 187-188n
Scopes "Monkey trial," 184, 224-25, 226
Sea Island cotton, 17
Sherman, William T., 25n, 101
short-line railroads, 33, 60, 158-59, 249-50
Simmons, William J., 151-52, 154
slaves: historic numbers of, 21; in cotton production, 17
slavery: growth due to cotton culture, 21; historic moral ambiguity of the North, 21-23
small towns in Georgia: life in, 12-14; population sizes in 1900, 32; social structure, 12
Stone Mountain Confederate Memorial Association, 184
Stowe, Harriet B., 30
sweet potatoes,16
Tanner, J. J., ("Jim"), 188, 192, 193, 195, 251; indicted for murder, 206. *See also*: murder trials
Tanner, Ralph Rawlings, 235
Tarbutton, Benjamin J. ("Ben"), 86, 103, 137, 180, 213, 249
Tarbutton, Fluker, 187, 188, 190-92, 197, 203, 213, 223, 224, 227, 230, 233, 241.
Tarbutton, George Augustus ("Gus"), 5, 93-95, 105, 175, 267; details of death, 188-91; death of wife, 180; funeral, 192-194; investigation of death by Coroner's jury, 192-93; involvement in Letcher Tyre

killing, 47-57. *See also*: murder trials
Tarbutton, Herschel V.: involvement in Letcher Tyre killing, 47-57
tenant farming, 68, 144, 167-168; development of system, 27-29; payment arrangements, 28-29; tenants, 29, 168
Temperance movement, 42-43, 121
Tennille, 10-11, 13, 60, 64, 140, 158, 178, 185, 250
Terrell, Joseph M., 56
The Birth of a Nation, 101
timber sales, 175
Tyler, Elizabeth, 152
Tyre, J. B., 52
Tyre, J. Letcher, 47-57
United Daughters of the Confederacy, 184
Washington County, 9-11, 18, 28, 58-59, 65, 86, 92, 100, 101. 108, 132, 154, 159, 164, 170, 173, 185, 221, 247, 248, 250
Watson, Thomas E., 50, 155, 156
Wesson Oil, 16
Whitney, Eli, 15; (re)invention of cotton gin, 17-18
World War I: effect on cotton prices, 80, 87, 93, 96, 109; German spies in Georgia, 100-101, 111; local view of, 86, 96, 99-100
Wray, William Arthur, 121, 137, 158, 166, 173-74, 177, 180, 182, 193, 213